ALL MY EDENS

All My Edens

A Gardener's Memoir

BY PAT WELSH

CHRONICLE BOOKS

SAN FRANCISCO

Printed in the United States.

Book and cover design: Ursula Brookbank

Library of Congress Cataloging-in-Publication Data:
    Welsh, Pat.
    All my edens : a gardener's memoir / Pat Welsh.
    p. cm.
    Includes index.
    ISBN: 0-8118-0904-8
    1. Welsh, Pat. 2. Gardeners—United States—Biography.
    3. Gardeners—England—Biography. 4. Welsh, Pat—Homes and haunts—California
    —Del Mar. 5. Gardening. I. Title.
    SB35.W.39A3   1996
    635.9'092—dc20
    [B]   95-14623
                                                                    CIP

Distributed in Canada by Raincoast Books,
8680 Cambie Street
Vancouver, B.C. V6P 6M9

10   9   8   7   6   5   4   3   2   1

Chronicle Books
275 Fifth Street
San Francisco, CA 94103

Chronicle Books® is registered in the US Patent and Trademark Office.

BACK COVER TOP In my garden, 1995.

BOTTOM I took up gardening at an early age. Here I am, aged three, with my hands in the soil at Hoyle Court.

TITLE PAGE Chess Cottage, 1934. The author at five years of age dressed as a woodland fairy in nothing but flowers.

Acknowledgments

SOME PASSAGES IN this book have appeared previously in *San Diego Home Garden Magazine.* I'm grateful to Peter Jensen, who was the editor during most of the years when I was there, for suggesting the idea for this book. I also want to thank my beloved family—my husband Louis and our children and grandchildren—for their continual encouragement and support. Additionally, I thank all those friends and relations who have so kindly permitted me to use their names in this book.

Many other friends and relations, including Loretta Foreman, Virginia Lott, Carole Carden, my cousin Harriet Bemus, and my brother John Fisher-Smith have helped in various ways. Anne Spadea provided facts and photos regarding her parents' houses, gardens, careers, and guests. I also thank the members of the Del Mar Garden Club. Their kindness and enthusiasm, their ways of weaving beauty into their lives, and their expertise in the garden have enriched my life and this book.

I am grateful to my agent Sandra Dijkstra for her faith in this book and to Rita Holme from the Dijkstra Agency for her help and enthusiasm. My editor, Charlotte Stone, at Chronicle Books has been a joy to work with; no writer could ask for more kindness or understanding. Additionally, I thank Chuck Robbins, copy editor, for his helpful contributions; Ursula Brookbank for her stunning design; and Amy Torack for her creative publicity.

Contents

Dedication

WITH LOVE TO my children and grandchildren—

Francie and Peter Filanc, Yvette and Erica;

Wendy and Larry Woolf, Rebecca, David, and Rachel.

INTRODUCTION

In Memory's Garden

O thou, that dear and happy isle,
The Garden of the World erewhile,...
What luckless apple did we taste
To make us mortal and thee waste?

Andrew Marvell

MY GARDEN IS nestled on a hill in Southern California, less than half a mile from the sea. The ocean is to this garden what the Japanese would call its "borrowed scenery," a distant view incorporated into the garden's design. The sight of it is a daily reminder that Southern California's proximity to the Pacific Ocean combined with a location on the southwest corner of a giant continent gives us our Mediterranean climate with its moderate temperatures, dry summers, and winter rains. This mild but dry climate cements our spiritual bond with gardeners around the world who tend their plants in climates similar to ours—gardeners in Italy, Greece, southern France, and the coastal sections of all the other countries that border on the Mediterranean Sea, as well as gardeners in Chile, South Africa, and southwestern Australia.

In my garden the ocean is a constant companion. When the sun shines, as it does more often than not, you can see the ocean in the blue of shadows and hear it in the distant roar of breaking waves. When fog draws a drippy curtain across the view, as it sometimes does for a month or more, it muffles every sound except the sea's. At night the ocean's sound is magnified, and every pounding wave is like a heartbeat drifting up our canyon to wash over you and take away the day's grime.

Today the sun is out, and "the surf is up," as surfers say when the waves are six to eight feet high and perfect for riding. The boom of the combers as they curl over and tumble onto the beach makes me glad to be alive here and now in my Southern California garden. Sometimes, though, it seems as if the present has all the past wrapped up inside it, as if all the gardens I've gardened in before and all the gardeners I've ever known continue to live in some form or other within this place and time. For like so many other local gardeners, I've not always lived and gardened here.

England of the 1930s was my introduction to the love of nature and of gardening. I was born in 1929—the year of the stockmarket crash—into a family of Yorkshire manufacturers and avid garden lovers in Halifax, West Riding, Yorkshire, a district of moors and mills in the north of England. Later, I lived for a while in the south of England in a thatch-roofed cottage surrounded by woods. After the family emigrated to America, there were other times and places too that shaped my vision of nature and of gardening: a tree-filled garden on Long Island; an apple orchard in Nyack, New York; a palm forest in Daytona Beach; an island off the coast of Maine; a farm in Pennsylvania. Each offered totally different soil and climate—some better, some worse than I confront here. Then in the mid-forties, I moved to Hollywood. Since then I've lived and gardened in Inglewood, Malibu, Claremont (at the foot of Mount Baldy in the San Gabriel Valley), and finally Del Mar.

Nor has this garden or this neighborhood always been the way it is now. In the thirty-nine years since Lou and I built our home and raised our children here, there've been many changes: an increase in population, more houses, much more traffic, and so many more people on the beach that it seems as though the Southern California I once knew has metamorphosed into a strange land. Even gardening has become unaccountably different than I expected it always to be.

When this sense of life's increasing complexity strikes, I yearn for simpler times and long-remembered places and the many and varied characters, especially the gardeners, who peopled those times and places and taught me so much of what they knew. So, though this book is about gardening in Southern California, it's also about all those other gardens that preceded this one, and the fascinating people with whom I've shared and continue to share a passion for plants.

But scratch nostalgia and you can often see through it; things weren't necessarily better then than now. For example, years ago I never sat down to relax and muse like this in my garden because its imperfections loomed more vividly to me than its virtues. Every neglected task became a nag, every faded flower a rebuke. Real gardeners never sit in their gardens, I thought; they only work in them. Now I've discovered I was wrong—or else perhaps I'm no longer a real gardener. (What a relief!)

Imperfections don't bother me so much and everything seems more beautiful. Today, if a cosmos needs deadheading, I enjoy the warblers who visit it for seeds. If they knock it down, I may prop it up again but perhaps not. I confess I can't see the faded flowers quite as clearly as I once did. When I get totally myopic, I just may sit in my garden like Monet and paint huge pictures.

This occurred to me a few minutes ago while I slouched, totally relaxed, feet propped up on a forty-year-old redwood stool—remnant of those innocent days when we didn't stop to consider what manner of tree was felled to provide our patio furniture. I was leaning with my head back on the striped cushion of an old chair, eyes half closed, mind drifting. I was not asleep but in that super-awake state that can happen in spring when, besides the sea, only the birds are heard, and people and all the trappings of surburban life—cars, trucks, barking dogs, airplanes—for one brief, happy moment fall silent.

It's said that in the eighteenth century people gardened to recreate Eden and recapture the bliss of Adam and Eve before they ate the apple. Now, in the last gasp of the twentieth century, I plant wildflowers to replace all my lost Edens. Fifteen years ago, I could ride a horse all the way from the canyon behind Del Mar to Black Mountain ten miles inland and never see another person, sometimes not even another house. In spring wildflowers covered the hills. Yellow dogtooth violets abounded in shady spots and summer-deciduous ferns clothed the northfacing walls of gullies in a green fur coat. Sycamores graced the canyons, and in one place, a stream ran year-round. Now the backcountry is full of houses, the native plants have been replaced by golf greens, the hilltops have been bulldozed flat for nurseries and shopping centers, and I plant bright California poppies, blue larkspur, and scarlet flax to remind me of wild places. In full flower on this March morning, their vivid colors push against my half-closed lids and snap them open.

Higher on the hill, beyond the roses, a great splash of purple wisteria drips from the pergola that covers a brick path leading to our front door. There's a story about that wisteria, but it can wait. Looking back from here it seems that life has been rather like that vine and the path too, an interwoven pattern of tendrils and byways tying gardens and incidents and people together into a continuing story. Paths led the way through time and space, creating connections. Vines wound through every garden like the interweaving incidents of life. People were attached to plants and to gardens, twining, reaching, connecting, continuing to grow. Plants and stories, all growing like Jack-in-the-Beanstalk's fable from seeds that became plants that then became trees and shrubs and flowers and vegetables and vines, tying and retying events into patterns of growth, fulfillment, loss, and retrieval.

This book, also, is like a vine with many twiners going this way and that. It doesn't begin at the beginning of the story or end with the end of it. Nonetheless, wound through this book, like the vine's main trunk, is the tale of my plant-oriented childhood in England and America and how my immigrant family went from riches to rags on the road to becoming established in this country. All my life I've been telling bits and pieces of this story. Someday, I meant to write it all down. I never found just the right vehicle until one day when I was having lunch in our garden with my friend Peter Jensen. "Why not do a book containing all your stories?" he suggested. "Put them down just as they occur to you, not chronologically, and wind them together with gardening." The next day I sat down to write this book, and I've enjoyed every minute of it.

SOME ELEMENTS OF DESIGN

1.

The Path That Peter Built

WHENEVER YOU ENTER a garden, whether by a gate, across a lawn, or through a shrubbery, your steps will almost always be guided by a path. Immediately you can guess something about the garden, perhaps even about the gardener. Paths dictate the style and spirit of a garden. Winding paths are informal, while straight or geometric ones are formal. Paths tie together the design of a garden and outline many of the shapes in it. They lead to buildings, views, focal points, garden rooms, and hidden secrets. They're a way for the gardener to take visitors by the hand and say, "Come this way, there's something I want to show you."

That being so, it's strange that the first example of a garden path to pop into my mind is, or was, an ugly one. It ran downhill at an awkward angle, cutting diagonally across the sloping lawn below the herbaceous border in front of the Gleddings, my grandmother Lady Hattie Fisher-Smith's house in Halifax, Yorkshire, England. This path was neither straight nor gracefully curved; it was kind of a cross between the two, but my brother John and I loved it. We often careened down it in a miniature Conestoga

wagon, a remnant of Dad's childhood that we'd found in the attic. It was a real challenge not to capsize and tumble out onto the scruffy lawn.

Dad's mother, our Grandma Hattie, was a charming American from Boston whose interests ran more to politics and philanthropy than to gardening. During the last years of her life, Grandma was in a wheelchair. All the paths in her garden, including the one that sliced across the lawn, were surfaced in crushed, compacted cinders so that Grandma, whose size was as generous as her disposition, could be wheeled about. No one can deny that every garden path should be as beautiful as possible, but it's even more important for them to work.

ABOVE My paternal grandparents, Sir George and Lady Hattie Fisher-Smith hosting a garden party at the Gleddings. OPPOSITE As my parents strode through this arch, which led from the courtyard to the west terrace at Hoyle Court on their wedding day in 1923, it looked like smooth sailing ahead. Who could have guessed that the Great Depression would add their marriage to its wreckage?

I confess that some of the paths in my California garden are more beautiful than practical. They're built of brick laid in sand, and parts are shady enough for a slippery layer of moss or algae to gain a foothold in wet weather. We use a long-handled brush and a solution of half a cup of bleach to half a bucket of water to scrub off the algae, but it's a bother. Brick laid in cement doesn't grow moss as readily as sand-laid brick because the cement dries out more quickly after rain.

Despite the moss problem, brick has many virtues: it's elegant, affordable, warm in color and texture, easy to install, and adaptable to many garden styles. Additionally, brick can be laid in a variety of interesting patterns. A narrow side yard in San Francisco is lifted above the ordinary by a snake-like path of end-laid bricks that undulates down the side of the house, culminating in a wide loop that spirals to a center, thus forming a unique circular patio. A palm garden created by Ed Moore in Pacific Beach, a district of San Diego, is interlaced with narrow brick paths that wind in and out of an enchanted forest and lead to hidden patios bordered by fountains, pools, and waterfalls. Ed laid old bricks straight into the sandy soil, arranging them in the basket weave pattern—two parallel bricks in one direction and the next two at right angles to them. "When a plant invades a path," he says, "I simply move the path over, to make room. That's why the paths branch and turn."

Some paths don't seem to lead anywhere in particular, but nonetheless have a special function. Richard and Sue Streeper, eminent rosarians who live in La Mesa, California, have a smooth, wide, and beautifully constructed cement path that makes a complete loop around their home and swings in a broad arc through their rose-filled backyard. I knew there had to be a special reason for the shape of this path, so I asked.

"Oh," Richard laughed, "I built that as a sort of freeway for our three sons and their friends when they were little. While Sue and I worked with our roses they happily rode their tricycles around and around the house for hours on end."

"It went through stages," added Sue. "First, it was little kids pushing their Tonka trucks. Then they grew into trikes and wagons and windup cars, and finally roller skates and bikes—anything with wheels, and it lasted for years."

The late Bill Gunther's garden in my own hometown of Del Mar is a unique example of path-making as garden design and folk art combined. It began as a way to stabilize a cliff. Bill and his friends built a structure of wandering paths of rock, rough cement, and tile that meanders all over what was once a steep cliff face. Between the paths a network of fountains and water-filled ponds drains down the cliff. Palms, bromeliads, and many other exotic plants live in rock-walled raised beds filled with mushroom compost.

"Children love this place," Bill once told me. "First, they silently explore, and pretty soon they start running round on the paths, chasing each other, and shrieking with delight."

Grandma Hattie's path—the one that sliced diagonally across the lawn—was a path that purposefully led somewhere. If you followed it beyond the lawn and through the rhododendrons, you came at last to a gate in the seventeenth-century stone fence that walled the sheep pasture. Perhaps this path had been in use for hundreds of years. Originally, it may have been a deer track, a cow path, or a sheep trail. Most grazing animals walk uphill the easiest way, at an angle, flattening the ground as they go, exactly the shape of Grandma's path. I can imagine it as a track used by falconers on horseback in the Middle Ages. (In those days a falcon field was called a gleddings.) The field probably became a pasture when the stone fence was built, and finally, in the nineteenth century, after the house was erected, it became a lawn. Most likely through all the changes, the angle of that path remained exactly where grazing animals had first put it centuries ago. There are thousands of paths like that in England, some dating from Roman times. Regardless of its looks, Grandma's path was heavy with a sense of place and atmosphere, even romance.

Equally alluring is an ancient Hawaiian lava trail leading through a bamboo forest to a hidden waterfall or a Pennsylvania garden path that winds through woods to an old springhouse and is edged on each side by hostas, azaleas, primroses, and violets. But in my garden overlooking the Pacific, I'm not so interested in achieving tropical or cold-climate effects as I am in capturing the essence of the Mediterranean atmosphere so appropriate to our dry, sunny climate. Brick patios and wandering

A FAVORITE PHOTO of mine and thus very worn. This is the way Hoyle Court looked when we left for America. You can see the vegetable gardens over the wall in the background.

paths have long ago taken the place of lawns. In an informal area where wildflowers and vegetables grow, I've covered the paths with a layer of mulch delivered free from a local tree-trimmer.

Decomposed granite packed down hard is another practical path material for informal areas in western gardens. It's no good for slopes. Unlike rolled cinders, it washes out. But where the ground is flat it blends well with drought-resistant plants and is in keeping with California's Spanish heritage and the look of old mission gardens, especially if you edge it with rocks, adobe bricks, or abalone shells. Tile paths express the Mediterranean look particularly well in formal gardens, while flagstones are complimentary to almost any architectural or garden style.

I can't think of flagstones without remembering the gardens at Hoyle Court, a Queen Anne–style house built in 1910 by my grandfather Sam Ambler in Baildon, Yorkshire. Here I spent much of my early childhood during the Depression after my fun-loving father's various business disasters forced us to move back in with my mother's family. My brother John and I now had a huge house to clatter about in; the upstairs hall was so long and wide that we were allowed to play football there on rainy days. Of course, we plaid English football (soccer); we tried not to kick the ball high enough to hit the dark, eighteenth-century portraits that lined the walls. Some of the rooms were locked up because the Ambler family was rapidly losing its fortune, but unlike the Gleddings, which was so crushed full of furniture and china that you could hardly move without knocking something over, Hoyle Court was furnished in impeccable taste.

At times my headlong dash to keep up with John was brought to a screeching halt by something so beautiful I just couldn't rush past it. Once it was two glass urns on inlaid stands higher than a man—one on either side of a door—with sprays of pink climbing roses cascading down from them almost to the floor, filling the hall with fragrance. (Viney, the kindly head gardener, was also a master flower arranger.) Another time it was a single ray of sun lighting on a painting of fringed and nodding tulips, and a real bee buzzing in front of them. There were no window screens in that house or any other English house I ever lived in; bees wandered in and out—birds too sometimes.

As was common in those days, the house had its share of live-in servants, including a cook, a scullery maid, three housemaids, and our nurse Norah—a skeleton staff compared with the number of servants before the crash. Nonetheless, every day except Sunday the halls and stairs were vacuumed before nine A.M., and the linen sheets were changed on all the beds. The property had its own laundry in a separate building next to

TOP Mum, John, and I in 1932 on the wall next to the steps that led from the courtyard to the rose garden at Hoyle Court.

ABOVE Gran Ambler, John, Norah, Pat, and Dad having tea in the gardens of Hoyle Court in August 1932. During the Depression Dad's business reverses forced my parents to move in with her parents. I was three.

WHILE STUDYING PAINTING in Paris, Aunt Elizabeth fell in love with the great American portrait painter Robert Henri. Grandma wanted to "look him over" so commissioned him to paint this 1907 portrait of her wearing the mayorial jewels of the town of Halifax, borrowed for the occasion. (Grandpa and Grandma were Mayor and Mayoress in the 1890s.)

the kitchen where two or three women came from Baildon village six days a week to wash and iron. Also on the property was the farmhouse where the farmer, the farmer's wife, and the farmer's boy lived. Viney and Mrs. Viney lived in the gatehouse at the bottom of the drive; the under-gardeners lived in Baildon. Since the crash, the Amblers had given up their chauffeur; when they needed a driver they got one from the mill. Grandad commuted to work by train. Baildon Station was just above the garden, and wonderful black steam engines chugged by many times a day. The train tracks were cut down below the level of the ground. From the house you could barely hear the trains whistle; all you could see was their smoke.

Best of all, John and I now had an enormous garden with many mys-terious "rooms" to explore and play in and a wild and lovely moor with-in easy walking distance. The gardens included two orchards carpeted with daffodils in spring, a topiary, a walled formal garden centered by an oblong lily pond surrounded by Italian statues, an overgrown tennis court, a vegetable garden, several greenhouses, a courtyard, a farm with farm animals, and a hayfield. There was even a small zoo with tropical birds, tropical fish, a foul-mouthed green parrot that Grandad had bought from a sailor—it lived in the kitchen—and a bad-tempered monkey called Gretchen, who had once bitten the postman. John and I gave her smelly cage a wide berth. All else—or almost all—delighted us.

The attic at Hoyle Court also yielded its treasures, remnants of the childhoods of heroic Uncle Ted, killed in the First World War, our beau-tiful mother Ruth, and handsome Uncle Jack. John hoisted the creeky lid of an old trunk and found it filled almost to the brim with whole armies of lead soldiers. We discovered a Swiss farm set, each piece wrapped care-fully in tissue, the best toy I ever had. Beneath a dusty sheet, we uncov-ered a miniature, beautifully painted Italian street organ, with wheels, handles, and a crank—useful for costume parties, we decided, if only we had a smaller and tamer monkey. Finally, we stumbled on a child-sized toy canoe with two paddles inside it and wheels attached to the bottom.

John wanted to float the canoe in the lily pond. "No!" I said. "It will sink." But John said, "I don't want a stupid canoe with wheels; I want a real one I can paddle in my pond." I tried to talk him into taking the canoe into the courtyard and pretending it was a lake. The paths could be streams, the orchard a forest filled with deer, and we would be "Red Indians." (Like many English children, we were crazy about Indians; no one called them Native Americans in those days.) We argued at the top of our lungs as we wrestled the ungainly canoe with the paddles rattling around inside it down the attic stairs, through several doors, down the circular staircase, past the grandfather clock, out into the garden, and—because John was three years older—across the terrace, down the terrace steps, and finally, with a great splash, into the lily pond.

If Mum had been there, she would have stopped us, but Mum and Dad were away—yachting around Scotland, perhaps, which my photo albums show they often did. Gran and our nurse Norah, the strict disciplinarians, where were they? Perhaps they were restrained by Grandad or Uncle Jack, who believed in many types of mischief. So, left to our own devices we clambered quickly into the canoe. "Paddle!" yelled John. "As fast as you can!" As usual, he was the chief, and I was the Indian. "But we're sinking!" I cried. "Then BAIL, idiot!" shouted John.

I cupped my small hands and threw water out as fast as I could, but not fast enough. The canoe sank, and one or two of Viney's gardeners who'd been pruning a row of espaliered pear trees leaped off their ladders and came running and laughing to pull us and it out of the pond. John and I were muddy but unscathed. The canoe would never be the same.

Sometimes John and I crossed the wooden footbridge that led over the railroad tracks and wandered through "the snicket" and up onto the open moor that was yellow with gorse in spring and stained purple with sweet-smelling heather in summer. The snicket was a narrow path between two

THE WALLED FORMAL garden at Hoyle Court was centered by a lily pond surrounded with Italian statuary, including one of Venus in the middle. The Yorkshire flagstones had *Armeria maritima* and a delightful collection of alpine plants growing in them, many of which were aromatic. These plants, as well as flowers spilling out of urns and impeccably designed herbaceous borders backed by roses, are clearly visible here. As a child playing in this garden I became willy-nilly a garden snob and mentally criticized the herbaceous borders at the Gleddings which I loved for their fun aspects but which didn't compare with Hoyle Court's borders either in design or elegance.

walls containing ancient stone steps worn deep through centuries of use. Halfway up, a clear spring bubbled into a trough cut from a huge block of rock. Other days we climbed into the apple trees, taking books to read like Mum had told us she and her brothers used to do. But we didn't take puppies to piddle all over us like they did. Sometimes we rode our tricycles and later our bicycles around and around the courtyard, breaking up the oily rainbows that floated on all the puddles while we listened to Chopin or Rachmaninoff or Beethoven floating out to us from the music room where Gran was practicing on the Steinway grand piano Grandad had given her for a wedding present. (It was her passionate way of playing that had made him fall in love with her.) And once we hid between box hedges, smoking clay pipes filled with "tobacco" made from rolled corrugated cardboard—one of John's least inspired inventions.

Many times we dogged Viney's steps all day long. While he pretended not to look, we crawled up the cinder path through the vegetable garden to steal his luscious pink gooseberries. For some reason these were forbidden fruit—perhaps to make us like them? The cinders cut my knees, but John insisted we must crawl. The fun part began after we'd filled our hands and pockets with plump squishy fruit and John stood up with a taunting laugh. Then Viney, feigning anger, grabbed a garden rake and chased us up and down the garden paths but never caught us.

At Hoyle Court all the paths on the terrace and walled garden were of flagstone from a local quarry. Lichen grew on them, and some held little puddles after rain. If flagstones aren't laid just right, people may trip. At Hoyle Court there were additional reasons for tripping. The gaps between the stones were planted with the most marvelous collection of rare alpine plants, including many smooth-domed miniature dianthus, English lavender, candy tuft, wallflowers, and thrift.

I've tried several times to get thrift to grow in my Southern California garden because it's charming, drought-resistant, and for me redolent with memories, but it refuses. A friend of mine who lives in Oceanside planted thrift between stepping stones on the north of her house, and there it thrived. If you want people to notice a small but choice plant in your garden, place it near a stepping stone. Stepping stones aren't suitable for paths leading to front doors; they require too much attention. The great value of stepping stones, other than their adaptability to artistic arrangement and the ease of installing them, is the fact that they slow us down so we watch and listen and look.

Years ago I was building a winding path of square stepping stones here in my Southern California garden. I was laying the stones diagonally point to point down a slope and filling the triangular spaces on each side of them with smooth blue-gray beach rocks. A young man called Peter who was sixteen years old and dating our eldest daughter Francie, also sixteen, came down the path and stood over me.

"What are you doing?" he asked.

"Making a path. Though I guess in my mind I'm really building a grandchildren's garden. Someday I'll have grandchildren, so I'm making wandering paths for them to run round on and enjoy. But now I see I'll never finish because I don't have enough rocks."

"I have a truck," he said. "I'll get you some."

The next day that young man showed up at dawn to collect my daughter. Together they spent all day gathering blue-gray beach rocks—no law against it in those days where they went. That night they brought me a truck full of rocks, enough to finish the path.

Many years have passed, and the garden has undergone many changes. But there's still a grandchildren's garden, and now there are five grandchildren to play in it. And what of that young man who helped me build my path? He went off to school and then he traveled the world. Eventually, he came home again, married Francie, and gave me the first two grandchildren to go in the garden.

A MAGNIFICENTLY GROWN
row of delphiniums flanking a flagstone
path at Hoyle Court, apparently edged
with thyme. My grandfather was particularly fond of aromatic plants spilling
over onto paths so they would give off
their fragrance when one accidentally
stepped on them.

2.

Gardeners Who Paint with Flowers

SOMETIMES YOU KNOW immediately when you're in the presence of a great gardening talent. That's the way I felt one hot afternoon in late spring when I first visited Karen Kees's cottage garden in Poway. In the distance stood the Kees's rustic California cottage set high on its foundation of native granite boulders. In front, a winding path of flagstones and gravel invited us to explore a maze of mounded beds planted with an exciting array of perennials, bulbs, herbs, and annual flowers. A strong design sense held all the plantings together, but left them natural and unstrained.

Everywhere I looked flowers bloomed, and thanks to a thick layer of mulch, nothing wilted. At the far end of the garden, we wandered past a great drift of daylilies, then around the house past a patch of Mexican primroses and a dramatic clump of Matilija poppies, then through an arch overgrown with Japanese wisteria. Karen had chosen these and other plants—lamb's ears, annual gomphrena, and a wide collection of South African bulbs—for their drought-resistance and ability to stand up well to heat. Nothing was crowded, yet there weren't any ugly gaps staring at you like missing teeth.

The afternoon lives in my memory like one of those photos on a greeting card that makes you feel as if you could walk straight into it. Eventually we settled into wicker chairs on the front porch, and sipped iced tea while I scribbled down our conversation on a yellow legal pad. I was planning to tape a TV show spotlighting Karen's garden and wanted to learn more about its creator. I knew Karen had been a painter of considerable merit until all at once her life had changed direction.

"Suddenly everything was gardening," she said.

"You got bitten by the gardening bug!"

"I guess I did. And then the garden just naturally led me into a career as garden designer. Everything happened by accident, but just as if it had been planned."

"Your garden has no lawn. Is that a philosophy of yours? I mean did you skip the lawn to cut down on irrigation?"

"Flowers use no more water than a lawn, and I'd rather have flowers," she explained, "But this was nothing new. I'd always wanted flowers instead of a lawn because I was greedy for color. Mike and I have no children to play on a lawn—the best reason for having one—and our dog seems just as happy on the paths."

I asked Karen if she'd drawn a plan for her garden, but she said, "It just sort of evolved." And when I told her I admired her color sense but couldn't figure out how she did it, she laughed. "No one ever can! I'm not one of those gardeners who stick to a particular color scheme—I don't have a specific formula—so perhaps it isn't easy to see how it's done. I simply place plants where I think they're going to grow best and fit into the available space. If something doesn't look right, I move it! I garden by the seat of my pants—actually by my muse. When people look at the result, it seems spontaneous, not thought out in a formal way. But the truth is I had a vast knowledge of plants, sizes, and forms before I began. This isn't my first garden. I've gardened most of my life, so I pretty much knew what I wanted, but I had to try it out."

"Your background as a painter must have taught you a lot about color."

"I think any painter who becomes a gardener benefits from the knowledge of how colors work together, and this is part of it. But I also have a very broad ability to accept color combinations, so I'm not afraid to make mistakes. People who are afraid of color have to be careful, but most of the time I'm not overly cautious. Willingness to make a mistake is very important. 'Take chances!,' I tell people. 'Don't be afraid to do your own thing!'"

The late Alice Menard of Lakeside, California, was at the opposite end of the spectrum. She left nothing to chance. Around her small World War II–vintage cottage masses of brilliant annual and perennial blooms spilled out of flowerbeds that surrounded a well-manicured lawn of coarse, heat-loving St. Augustine grass. Iceland poppies, pinks, candy tuft, snapdragons, larkspur, paludosum daisies, nemesia, linaria, and ranunculus were laid out in drifts backed by shrubs and a rose-covered fence. Clumps of tall spiky flowers were meticulously arranged among others with more rounded or flowing shapes. Each group of plants had adequate space, but there wasn't one spot of bare ground. It looked as if a professional English estate gardener had done the job, so I assumed that Alice had formal training.

"Where did you learn how to do this?" I asked

"Right here!" she answered with a grin, spreading her arms wide. "It just comes naturally. And no one taught me how; I just do it. I lay out my spring garden in October and November, setting out my bedding plants from flats I've grown from seeds planted in August. But my family were English people who came to California in the nineteenth century.

A VIEW OF Alice Menard's rose garden, edged with annual flowers grown from seeds.

I remember my grandmother's garden in the San Gabriel Valley. She grew the most beautiful roses and iris and other flowers all in drifts. You should have seen her spring bulbs! So I guess it's in the blood."

Even Alice's exuberant rose garden at the far end of the property was carefully planned.

"It was that pink one, Century Two, that got me into all the trouble," she laughed. "Prior to that I had only a dozen. Then all of a sudden the rose bug bit me. Soon I had 35 roses, and now I've got 125."

"And how did you make it look so harmonious?"

"I coordinate my colors for a better effect. In the first place practically no variety is represented by a single plant. I've got them all in threes, fours, and sixes. And I wanted a real show so I planted closely— about three feet apart. I also had picking in mind so I wound a path down the middle so I could work both sides."

We strolled down another path at the back of the rose garden while Alice pointed out the varieties. "I've got the orange roses like Bahia down at the south end of the bed divided off from reds such as Razzle Dazzle and Proud Land up here at the north end. I stayed away from lavender except for this one, Paradise. It's a beauty that turns a lot more pink than lavender, and has red tips that pick up the reds in the other flowers. See how I've placed it where it can help that white rose divide the oranges from the reds and the pinks? Next I put an orange salmon like Cathedral and then that brilliant hot orange Prominent. And then I go a step further and carry it through with the yellow Oregold next to that. Here and there I break it up with white, such as Evening Star. Then to make it charming I've edged my path with johnny-jump-ups, pansies, alyssum, Dutch iris, spring star flowers, and odds and ends. And of course I keep all the ground nice and neat and well mulched with bark because that saves water."

"But, nonetheless, you must have a hefty water bill."

"We don't talk about that!" laughed Alice. But in those days we still had plenty of water in Southern California, or so we thought.

"And do you have a specific color scheme?"

"I certainly do, and I even have a name for it. I call it the 'Sun Colors.' It's made up of the many shades of orange, yellow, gold, and red—all the colors of sunshine. These colors give my garden its bright happy look. I use very little pink and no lavender—I'm not a lavender person; it kills the effect. But I do splash in a little clear blue for the sky and lots of white to make all the colors sing. I think of my garden as a painting. White is the mat around the picture and the green lawn is the frame."

These two gardeners, Karen Kees and Alice Menard, and their contrasting philosophies of color and design, left a lasting impression on me and my garden. A year or two after meeting them, I began to create a new garden of my own for growing annuals and vegetables in full sun, a luxury I hadn't had for years. It began as a set for a television program, a place I could demonstrate garden tips year-round for my twice-weekly news segment on the local NBC station. In one part of the garden, I incorporated Alice's Sun Colors, but I knew I could never achieve her perfection—I'm far too slapdash for that. Karen's words "Take chances!" rang in my ears. I too wanted to plant with drought-resistance in mind, so I planted drifts right in the ground where I wanted the flowers to grow, using wild flowers and South African bulbs. The result was informal but exhilarating; a great deal had been left to chance, but it had worked.

People who have an innate sense of color and design don't need a color scheme, because the right combinations emerge naturally without the need for theorizing. I'm not one of them. I get better results when I give thought in advance to which colors blend and which don't. I almost always use some kind of color scheme when planting, but instead of adhering to just one system, I use several. I think it's fun to try out different color schemes in various parts of the garden. When I'm using bulbs, annuals, or container-grown plants, I may change my color scheme from year to year.

An example of a planting that has no real color scheme comes to mind, though it fits as perfectly in its location as an egg inside its shell. My husband Lou and I love to visit France where we sometimes rent a farmhouse that belongs to our friends, Cornel and Hilary Metternich. The farmhouse is two miles away from Pouillon, a *Village Fleuri* or flowered village. This is a special award given to French towns and villages that plant flowers on every available spot of ground not devoted to vegetables or lawn. Villages that rate this special appellation can display a small enameled sign advertising their status.

Pouillon sparkles with cleanliness and whitewash. Pink or red Balcon geraniums spill from urns and window boxes in front of every house and business. Massed flower beds surround the town square. Here's a sample recipe: One red-and-white variegated petunia, one orange African marigold, one pink ivy geranium, one white petunia, one red zonal geranium, one purple petunia, one pink semperflorence begonia, one yellow African marigold, one magenta zonal geranium. Zigzag these plants down the bed and repeat until the bed is filled.

The result dazzles you with color and stands up well to heat. Each plant screams for equal attention in a patchwork quilt that's not harmonious. But make no mistake about it, in Pouillon, I love these flower beds. I hope the townspeople never change them. Their unstudied exuberance is the perfect foil for the neat formality of a French village with its carefully manicured lawns, white walls, red tiled roofs, old church in the town square and heart-rending statue to "Our Fallen Heroes."

There is a similar look that works well here in the southwest, and it goes as well with Spanish architecture as Pouillon's patchwork goes with French. To achieve this effect, and an atmosphere of old Mexico, mix together all or several of the following colors: bright orange, vivid red, shocking pink, brilliant yellow, deep blue, and dark purple—bright clashing colors similar to those in Pouillon, but the difference is that you use larger masses or drifts of a single color, taking care to add great quantities of white, and omitting all variegated flowers. These look jittery and inharmonious; they prevent the eye from absorbing the entire scene. For example, you could splash a huge purple bougainvillea over a large white wall, throw in some pots of red geraniums and white alyssum and plant a bed of California poppies or orange gazaneas at their feet. The English have a word for such colors—garish—but they stand up well under our bright sun, which tends to wash out those muted shades that look so good in England.

Here's a game you can play that leads to one of the best color schemes for winter and spring. Begin by imagining the Patriotic Colors—red, white, and blue—a favorite color scheme in New England for filling tubs, window boxes, and leaky old row boats. Visualize, for example, a red geranium, some white sweet alyssum, and clump of bright blue ageratum. Now remove the red geranium and substitute a pink one; then add a pure yellow French marigold. Now you have pink, white, blue, and yellow—the Spring Colors. Use them to fill a pot or flower bed in spring or to brighten up the shade at any time of year. Add lavender to this color scheme, and it will look even better. Here and there you can even throw in a splash of red. My father, who was a painter, once told me, "Put a little blotch of red into every painting, and it will pull the whole composition together." But try not to use orange with the Spring Colors; it kills the effect in the same way that Alice Menard said lavender killed her Sun Colors.

If you've never gardened before and are starting out with bedding plants in bloom, try arranging them in your shopping cart to see which colors look best together. There are so many possible color schemes. You could, for example, recreate a rainbow from one end of a bed to the other, as has been done with orchids in an old historic garden high on a hill above Honolulu. I know gardeners who have copied the colors in a favorite fabric, painting, or photograph. Then there are the monochromatic gardens, all one color such as the Red or Blue Gardens in Bombay, or all white such as the White Garden at Sissinghurst—a soothing foil to Vita Sackville-West's violent passions.

White gardens are not as easy as they look. There are many shades of white, and some of them make others seem washed out if you put them side-by-side. (A clear white impatiens can make a white tuberous begonia look sick.) Some people love a lot of white. Others prefer saturated colors or soft pastel ones. My mother-in-law Frances Wright loved white flowers more than any other flower color and planted white geraniums all over her garden. But she had great trouble keeping them alive. In the end the sturdy old reds and pinks won out. I love white flowers—loads of them—as a contrast to set off and show up all the other colors in the garden. But too much white is as tiresome as too much color. In the current issue of *Garden Design* I happened across the words, "too much white in a garden is tiring on the eyes." Maybe it's because the color white gives off ultraviolet; that's what the bees see but our eyes can't. The article also said that white shines at night, especially on moonlit nights, so it should be put close to places that are seen in the evening.

I can't ignore the All Green Scheme—all the many colors of foliage. To do this well takes even more talent than white gardening. When Lou and I visited Stourhead, one of England's best-preserved eighteenth-century landscape gardens, we learned that it was one of the most noble of all foliage gardens until the latter part of nineteenth century when England was invaded by a flood of evil rhododendrons. These savage plants seduced Sir Henry Hoare, the sixth baronet of Stourhead, into shocking the horticultural aesthetes by fringing Stourhead's lakes with garish color. (There's that word again.) He even had the temerity to splash rhododendrons against Stourhead's classic temples. But Lou and I visited that garden when the rhododendrons were in bloom, and we were equally seduced. If you're a purist, be sure to visit Stourhead in very early spring or late summer, so you'll miss the show.

Some gardens need no color other than green. I'd seen postcards of the moss garden in Kyoto when the azaleas are in bloom, but when Lou and I visited Japan a couple of years ago I was satisfied by moss. If you want to see this garden you must write to the abbott two months in advance and ask permission. It's most important to arrive on the very dot of your appointment or the gates will clang closed. Then, before viewing the garden, one must take part in a Zen ceremony and meditation that lasts about an hour.

The best of all green gardeners is Mother Nature. Once, in the mid-1930s, I knew a garden so blessed by nature with one marvelous feature that it needed nothing else. I discovered this garden in the south of England shortly after my parents had moved to London to be close to Dad's newest business venture, a movie studio. At first all went well, so they bought land in a subdivided estate called Loudwater, near the town of Rickmansworth in Hertfordshire, and built Chess Cottage, a charming country house with a thatched roof. Shortly after we moved in, I made friends with a pleasant little boy who lived in a large house near the river. He was younger than me and not wildly interesting; it was his all-green garden I coveted.

This garden consisted of a lush green lawn, left rather long like a meadow that had been just slightly tamed. The glory of the garden was one of the river's crystal clear tributaries that snaked down the center of it between deep-cut banks. Two or three old pollarded willows—they could have been drawn by Arthur Rackham with faces on their swollen crowns and gnarled arms and hands—stretched their roots into the swift water and offered hiding spots to speckled trout. A path wandered here and there through the lawn, along the bank, and across the stream on wooden bridges with rails made out of willow branches. Eventually you came to a summerhouse with a rustic table and chairs inside and honeysuckle smothering its roof. Except for the yellow flags that grew in the stream and the English daisies that sprinkled the lawn, there were no other flowers in that garden; it didn't need them.

One final admonition about color: Don't forget the magic touch of gray. Once largely neglected, plants with gray foliage like dusty miller, lavender cotton, and blue fescue are now the rage. Gray goes well with bluish reds, lavenders, and all pastels. (Try putting pink cyclamen into a hanging basket of gray-leaved ivy.) Gray also can take the place of white. Use it to divide clashing colors or to make bright colors sing. I once planted a handful of orange Iceland poppies in front of a large clump of Spanish lavender. All winter and spring those poppies greeted me like a stream of sunshine breaking up a gray day. It had been a happy accident. The next time I put those two plants together, I'll do it on purpose.

PESTS, PROBLEMS,

GARDEN SKILLS, AND HELPERS

BUSINESS REPLY MAIL

First-Class MAIL   Permit No. 170   Marion, Ohio

POSTAGE WILL BE PAID BY ADDRESSEE

FATE

170 FUTURE WAY
PO BOX 1940
MARION, OH 43306-2040

3.

A Cottage in the Woods

I WAS FIVE YEARS old when we moved into Chess Cottage, and Norah and I set out through the gate from its woodsy garden to explore the surrounding countryside. We followed a footpath across a meadow fringed with primroses and into woods carpeted with bluebells and foxgloves. People have picked wildflowers so unmercifully that today there are few such places left, but in those days every open wood was a fairyland of flowers. Before long we came to a grassy clearing on the edge of which was a tiny brick cottage with a locked oak door and moss-covered roof. Norah thought it was a gamekeeper's hut built in Victorian times when Loudwater was still one vast estate. In the center of the clearing next to the hut was a circular patch of light green grass much shorter than the surrounding grass, as if little feet had worn it down. Inside the perimeter of this circle stood a perfect ring of golden brown toadstools glistening in the sunshine.

"A fairy ring!" cried Norah, and dropped her voice to a whisper. "I knew there were fairies in these woods. Gnomes too, probably. Here's

CHESS COTTAGE, with hollyhocks planted by Mum and Geoff. When I was a child I used to think the flecks of cinder in the bricks around the front door were in poor taste, another sign of the very strong opinions a child can pick up by osmosis. That memory helped me identify the house fifty years later when Lou and I went searching for it. It still looks just as good as the day it was built.

where they dance in the moonlight!" Although I was a gullible child, this time I had doubts, but bluebells and toadstools had certainly wrought a surprising change in the usually strict and practical Norah. "I'll prove it to you," she insisted. "We'll put out crumbs for them and come back the next day and see if they've gone. If they have we'll know for sure this wood is peopled with fairies."

That evening Norah gave me some squares of colored silver paper saved from a box of chocolates and showed me how to wrap them around the tip of my finger, twist them into the shape of long-stemmed goblets, and fill them with breadcrumbs. The next afternoon we found the fairy ring again and arranged the tiny goblets nearby on a patch of moss growing between the surface roots of an ancient beech tree.

When we returned the next day, all but one of our goblets had completely disappeared, and there wasn't a crumb to be seen. "See!" said Norah triumphantly. "The fairies took them, didn't they?" I asked, but secretly in my heart I thought the crumbs we put out had been taken by birds or perhaps by one of the many wild creatures who abounded in the woods and fields. As the days went by we often saw red squirrels, rabbits, hedgehogs, field mice, tortoises, and foxes, as well as signs that night creatures like stoats, weasels, or badgers had been busy when our backs were turned. Once we even caught sight of a rat—dead with a ghastly grin on its face—high up on a grassy bank beside the road. I craned my neck to get a better look, and got a long lecture from Norah

P.S.
I often think of
you coming up from
London to Hoyle Court,
clutching a piece of cotton wool,
made to look like a little white
mouse, + it was still in your
hand when we arrived

OPPOSITE In the garden at Chess Cottage my nurse,
Norah Widdop, teaching me to knit. I was all thumbs.
TOP I took up gardening at an early age.
ABOVE Long after I was married I got letters from Norah,
such as this one recalling one of our train trips to Hoyle Court.
RIGHT Chess Cottage, 1934. Me at five dressed as a
woodland fairy in nothing but flowers.

about the horrors of the Black Death.

While we were living at Chess Cottage, my brother John went to Beaumont House, a boarding school for boys. I attended kindergarten and later the first three forms at a little progressive school only a mile or two from home. This was the Rickmansworth P.N.E.U. school or Parents' National Educational Union. It emphasized fine arts, humanities, natural history, the Old Testament, and Shakespeare, all subjects I loved. When Miss Kitching, the headmistress, discovered I was hopeless at math, she said, "Never mind, we'll teach her later," a kindness I lived to regret. John, Norah, and I continued to go home to Hoyle Court by train for the holidays with our clothes packed in huge trunks. If we'd still been living in Yorkshire, I might have been sent to boarding school at the age of eight like poor John. Yorkshire families often sent their children to school in the south of England, so they wouldn't grow up with a North-country accent.

Lou and I visited the Rickmansworth P.N.E.U. school a few years ago and found it virtually unchanged. The entire student body was studying the Venetian painter Canaletto and putting the finishing touches on a production of *Twelfth Night*. Even the tiny gymnasium, with its climbing bars and leather tumbling horse, now cracked with age, was exactly as I'd remembered it.

After our visit, we set forth on foot under darkening skies to find Chess Cottage. It should have been only a mile or two away on the other side of the river, but unlike the school, the landmarks had changed. Fifty years ago much of the land was open and used for farming. Now there were houses everywhere, all the gardens were overgrown with trees, and the lovely views that had once existed were all hidden by foliage. The forest, cut down for fuel and farmland in the Middle Ages, was creeping back. When I was a child, a few ancient oaks and elms surveyed the surrounding countryside like lone sentries. Down in the valley, you could see the sparkling river and its meandering tributaries like blue veins on a giant green hand that was freckled with Golden Guernsey cows.

We crossed the main road where Lou spotted a rustic sign saying "Loudwater." Soon we came to the river and the bridge, but once on the other side we got lost in a maze of dirt roads. The woods got thicker, the clouds got darker, a few ominous raindrops began hitting our noses, and suddenly we were caught in a downpour. Even our umbrellas and raincoats weren't adequate protection. A taxi, splattering mud, bumped past with a passenger in the back seat. The driver gave us a broad smile and returned our frantic waves. In a few minutes he came back for us. "You've been looking in the wrong place!" he cried when he heard our story. "This is *new* Loudwater, developed after the war. You want *old* Loudwater. You crossed by the wrong bridge, see? But we're only a couple of miles off course. If your house is still standing I'll soon find it for you!"

The rain stopped, the sun came out, and soon we had found Chess Cottage. No one was home, and the name of the house was no help to us in identification—another cottage next to the river had usurped that. It was the facade that cinched it. I'd always remembered the bricks my mother had chosen for the wall on each side of the front door. They had little bits of glass and cinder baked into them—sort of a fake antique look—and I didn't like them. If only those bricks were plain, I used to think, it would look just like Snow White's cottage. But fifty years later I realized that, as usual in matters of taste, my mother was right.

The real problem with Chess Cottage was not the ornamental brick but the fact that, although Dad built the cottage for Mum, he never lived there. In 1934, shortly after we moved in, we suddenly had a new "Dad" called Geoff. Our real dad, Emerson Fisher-Smith, and his business partners had made three good motion pictures—*Tiger Bay* with Anna May Wong, *Men of Steel,* and *Alibaba and the Forty Thieves*—followed

ABOVE A movie still of my mother, Ruth Fisher-Smith, playing opposite Reginald Gardener, whom she did not like, in one of seven feature films produced in the early 1930s by my father.

LEFT Geoff always wore tweed jackets and smoked a pipe filled with pleasantly aromatic, navy-cut tobacco.

RIGHT A letter from my stepfather Geoff, remembering the early days of 1934. Photo of me at the zoo that Geoff refers to in the letter.

I remember & care for you most during those early years of 1934 & on. Can you still remember that sunny summer day that Ruth entrusted you to me & we

trotted happily up to the zoo together. Saw the effortants & the monkeys together. The moment in time that you squatted upon the low, broad retaining wall of the sea lions pool & I photographed your eager laughing face.?

I can. Vividly. And now, in the curious behavior of age, remember you better than I do when you I visited you at college. Took you & a couple of your friends out for a coke?.

Coming back to me. The plans for Germany still hold true. More so than before. I'll write you all about it . . . . . The Doctors tell me that I v visit there until late summm they make a prognosis that of vitality again.

As for v . . . . .

from. M. K. Morris
Sunny side
Old Buck

by four flops whose names I don't recall. Mum had starred in some of
them with Reginald Gardener. I was so proud of her I almost burst.
Despite that, the company went bankrupt, Dad's partners absconded to
France with the remainder of the funds, including a big chunk of
Grandma's fortune, and we were worse off than ever. This was the last
straw for Mum. She divorced Dad and married Geoffrey Morris, a fashion photographer who she hoped knew how to make a living. I learned
about this reason for the divorce years later. At the time no one
explained a thing to John or me because Mum didn't believe in making
excuses to children, and we knew we were not supposed to ask.

When I was in my teens, Dad said, "Your mother was too much of a
handful for me. If I'd been stronger I could have hung onto her." He
never stopped loving her, and his second wife Margot ("Maggie") never
seemed to mind. From then on Dad wandered in and out of our lives
and kept constantly in touch by letter and postcard. He traveled all over
the world, and wherever we lived, sooner or later, he showed up. When
Gran rented a seaside cottage so the family could go on a summer holiday, he took a room in the local pub, had a few too many, and remarked
amiably, "Have you seen that beautiful woman in the village with the
two children? Those are my kids and that's my wife!" After which all the
locals scowled at Geoff and Mum for the remainder of our stay.

Geoff roared into our family on a motorcycle. Like Dad, he was
handsome and dashing—he looked like a rugged Clark Gable. But
while Dad grew up in a happy family, Geoff grew up in an unhappy
one. At the age of sixteen, he had run away to sea. He was out of place
in a drawing room, and at his best outdoors. From now on, all our family parties were picnics and our weekends were spent gardening. No
longer did we have Viney and crew to do things for us; we did them
ourselves. Geoff was a bohemian, a sailor, a world champion rower, and
a fine artist. He was also a bundle of opposites—by turns, angry or

ebullient, rude or charming, strict or indulgent. You never quite knew where you stood.

Above all, Geoff was a gardener. No sooner had he moved into Chess Cottage than he'd trundeled in many a wheelbarrow full of manure, started a compost pile, filled the front garden with roses and delphiniums, and planted a vegetable garden behind the kitchen. (Even Norah approved of this.) Geoff quickly changed Mum from a movie star into a stonemason and with her help built a flagstone terrace surrounded by a low wall. "We have to give him credit," Mum said a few years ago. "He was a worker. He taught us all to work. Before that we were just playboys and girls; we didn't know how to do a thing."

I had to agree we learned a lot from Geoff, and I have much to thank him for. It was he who had chosen my school. Also, along with his motorcycle, his tweed jackets, his pipes, and the gold-plated Diamond Sculls cup he'd won at Henley, Geoff brought with him a model of the Santa Maria, Columbus's flagship. Unbeknown to the rest of us he'd already elicited a promise from Mum to emigrate to America.

It was just after Geoff had stormed into our lives that Norah told me there were fairies and gnomes in the woods around Chess Cottage. Perhaps she wanted to take my mind off John's absence and deflect my thoughts from my new stepfather. She needn't have worried. Despite Geoff's quick temper and unpredictability, I got along with him better than anyone else did. Besides, I'd found a new and secret source of security.

One golden afternoon when we were still living at Hoyle Court or spending a holiday there, I'd pushed through the little gate below the lily pond, slid down a bank beside the path, and discovered a small stream feeding a tiny pond. The water was crystal clear and surrounded by a sort of green grotto, every bit of it covered with moss. I was overwhelmed with delight. The voices of Gran, Mum, and Norah floated down to me from the terrace where they were sitting at the tea table. I dropped to my knees on the grassy bank beside the pond to be all alone in nature and hidden from view.

A small waterfall fell into the pond. On a round moss-coated rock under this waterfall sat a shiny green frog. It seemed to me that this place was sacred and that there had never been anything quite so beautiful. Time stood still. I was bathed by love, a deep understanding, and an awesome and comforting presence that went beyond words. I thought "This must be God." Then—splash!—the frog leaped into the water and swam straight towards me. The sudden sound destroyed the mood, but the memory remained.

After that experience I always felt happy and protected in the woods and fields. When I was old enough to know my way around Loudwater, Norah gave me freedom to wander. In many ways during the thirties, even though we all knew that we were soon to be visited by a terrible war, we felt surrounded by a safe world. Even children knew that difficult times lay ahead, but I only thought of that when I heard the grownups talking or saw worried looks on their faces as they huddled around the radio listening to the news.

At Chess Cottage the woods encroached so closely on the house that were it not for our wattle fence no one could have told where the woods stopped and our garden began. In winter wild birds sat on my hands to eat the breadcrumbs or suet Norah gave me for feeding them. I was only five when Gran Ambler had bought me six riding lessons with a local gypsy. For my sixth birthday she gave me a membership in the local pony club. One day a week I could ramble about on the back of "my" pony, Blackie, and imagine I was an American Indian. John and I had learned a great deal about them from the library at the Gleddings. On horseback I was a Plains Indian like those in Grandma's vellum-bound volumes of George Catlin's paintings, but on foot I was an Indian of the eastern lakes and rivers and hardwood forests, a noble savage straight out of James Fenimore Cooper—not a squaw, either, but a brave who hunted with a bow and arrow.

It was the totality of nature that filled me with bliss, not just the plants but the animals too. We were all one in some mysterious way and nature was composed of woods, fields, streams, wild animals, my pony, and me with the Great Spirit watching over all of us. Nature has a way of adopting children who need her attention. But as we grow up and come to live in more urban environments, we sometimes forget that the spirit of the biosphere, complete with its wild animals, still lives in our gardens.

In California I've often felt the throb of wildness in our canyons and on the hillsides. I've even tried to recapture that feeling in my own garden. But as an adult I've sometimes been less enthusiastic about the wild animals who are my garden's uninvited visitors. Intellectually I know they're as much a part of nature as the flowers, fruits, and vegetables, but sometimes, just like Shakespeare's Puck, they can make a lot of trouble.

4.

The Night I Saw a Gnome

SKUNKS, OPOSSUMS, RACCOONS, roof rats, mice, and gophers are just a few of the wild animals that flourish here in Southern California. They often live in close proximity to people who are oblivious to their presence. As long as that's the case, they're accepted. It's when wild animals become pests that their life hangs in the balance. It's easy to love wild animals when you're a child, and you don't have to cope with the results of their foraging. It's far more difficult when you're an adult to forgive a mole for ruining your lawn.

Luckily, if an opossum or a raccoon becomes a nuisance, you don't need to kill it. You can trap and release it in an unpopulated area or pay a professional to do the job. Skunks are more vexing because most extermination companies balk at handling them, as I discovered once when Lou was away on a business trip. There were more vacant lots around us in those days and so many skunks in our garden that I used to think we should call our place "Skunk Hollow." One day a confused skunk got under a large planter in the far corner of our atrium next to the front door and couldn't find its way out. I called several extermination companies but not one would help me. Finally, I rang the Del Mar Fire Department to see if they had any suggestions.

A few minutes later, a big red fire truck roared up the drive. Several laughing firepersons—three men and a woman—piled out of the truck carrying a large plastic trash can, a long bamboo pole, and a couple of brooms. "Official skunk-removal equipment," explained the Assistant Fire Chief in charge of the operation. "Now you'll see how brave we are. You go first!—Not you, Mrs. Welsh!—Tom here. He's new!"

Gales of laughter. You'd have thought a skunk caught in an atrium was the funniest thing in the world. The firemen put the trash can on its side, prodded the sleeping skunk awake with the bamboo pole, guided the befuddled creature into the can with the brooms, popped the lid tightly on the can, and upended the container. "We'll let it go in the slough!" they called as they hoisted the trash can on the truck and drove away. The whole operation had taken less than five minutes.

A couple of years ago, a skunk decided to hibernate in the narrow space under a wide shelf in my potting shed. I was upset, but Raymundo who helps me in the garden one day a week just laughed. "I'll smoke it out with my bee-keeper's smoke gun," he said. The next week he forgot to bring the smoker from Tijuana, so he squirted the skunk with the garden hose, a technique that worked equally well. Now I post signs: PLEASE CLOSE THIS DOOR TO KEEP OUT SKUNKS! Neither of these skunks left its calling card, but not all of our encounters have been as successful. Our standard poodle Max killed two skunks exactly one year apart on the same date—June 8—Lou's and my wedding anniversary. Max got tomato juice instead of champagne.

Skunks can be a nuisance, but they are beneficial. They dig up lawns and flower beds but eat great quantities of ground pests. You can stop skunks from defacing your lawn by controlling ground pests, such as

MAX IN OUR patio, 1969. John Lloyd Wright and I built the patio shade structure to shield our living room from the strong west sun.

white grubs, with beneficial nematodes or milky spore, a bacteria that kills the grubs of Japanese beetles. We don't have those in Southern California, but milky spore can also kill the larvae of rose chafer, Oriental beetle, and some May and June bugs that we do have. Milky spore works best on lawns; it's not as effective in flower beds. I protect my flowers from getting smashed down by skunks by wrapping the canes I prune from my climbing roses around the edges of the bed, like a low fence. The flowers soon hide the canes from view, but skunks know they're there and won't climb over them.

I have yet to meet a home gardener who feels that opossums are a serious threat to gardening. Other than a stolen apple or two and a few chewed-up tomatoes one hardly knows they exist. A local grower of cymbidium orchids, however, told me that opossums cause him considerable financial loss if not checked. "Possums relish the fresh young spikes of cymbidiums," he said. "I control 'em with poison bait. If I didn't I'd have no crop." The opossums in my garden walk past cymbidiums without even giving them a glance.

Raccoons are a mixed blessing. They rob birds' nests, fruit trees, and vegetable gardens, but they also eat snails and small rodents including mice and rats. A couple of years ago, Lou and I saw a large male raccoon gathering pine nuts on our roof. Knowing they're around, I usually wrap my apples in bird netting and tie them firmly to the tree. Last year I wanted to take a photograph of my young espaliered Anna apple tree after its apples had turned red. I got the photo, and something told me I should wrap and tie the apples immediately afterward. But it was a lovely day so Lou and I went to the beach. By the time we returned it was time to fix dinner. The next morning I got up early and went outdoors to wrap up the apples. Every one of them was gone. Those raccoons hadn't left me a single one!

Roof rats are almost everywhere in Southern California, particularly in old established neighborhoods where avocado, citrus, and macadamia trees provide them with an abundant food supply. You can love a raccoon, the little masked bandit of the garden, but there's nothing cute about a rat. Even rats, however, have one beneficial trait: they eat slugs and snails. Perhaps this is why people ignore their presence until they start driving the dog crazy or drowning in the swimming pool. Poisoning rats yourself can be tricky and dangerous especially if there are young children or pets in the family. In many areas rat extermination is free for the asking from the county vector control and even some pest-control companies.

One of the questions I'm asked most frequently is how to get rid of gophers. The obvious answer is to trap them. Easy to say when gophers had never yet invaded my garden. Then one morning last year, I walked down the garden path to see how my flowers and vegetables were doing. Right next to a magnificent row of parsley was a tell-tale mound of yellow sand. Through the years, I've added so much organic matter to the soil in my vegetable garden that the top twelve inches are rich dark-colored loam—almost black when wet. I knew that yellow sand must have come from far below.

Oh dear! Not a gopher, I hoped. But down in the canyon, wild land was being bulldozed and their homes were being destroyed. There was no hole, though. Maybe with luck the pile of sand had been made by a skunk. In the late afternoon, I checked the spot again, and now there was a fresh hole and little telltale paw marks in the sand. One huge parsley plant had totally disappeared, pulled—roots, leaves, stalks, and all—right down into the ground. What to do? It may sound ridiculous, but the first thing I did was sit down on the retaining wall and talk to the gopher.

"I'm warning you," I said, "if you don't leave I'll buy a gopher trap!" Then I went up to the house and told Lou what I was planning to do.

"I could never be a gardener," he said.

"Well, I lived on a farm. I had to butcher chickens, and I'm not about to give up vegetable gardening because of one little gopher."

Overnight I sent the gopher powerful thoughts to leave. He apparently got them, but instead of leaving he burrowed under the wall. I went to the nursery garden and bought a Blackhole Gopher Trap. It's said to work only on gophers and be safe around pets and children. It consists of a plastic tube that's open on one end and has a small hole in the other end to let in light and air. Inside there's a spring-loaded wire snare. You put the trap in the hole, the gopher comes charging along, smells fresh air or sees light ahead and runs right into the trap. That night I woke up with an uncomfortable feeling that I'd caught my gopher. Sure enough, next morning the trap was sprung and inside was one poor, dead, rather fat gopher. I hope that's the last one to invade my garden because I just might make friends with the next.

Sometimes it's not easy to deduce just which animal is damaging the garden. Once for a few moments I was convinced that the creature doing damage in the garden was not an animal at all but actually a gnome. This happened in the summer of 1948, the year after I'd graduated from Hollywood High and got a scholarship to Scripps College. No sooner was I out of the house than Mum and Geoff got fed up with Hollywood, where Geoff was working at the time, pulled up stakes, and moved back East again. They rented a studio in New York and bought a house called Woodhill in Bucks County, near New Hope, Pennsylvania.

It was a pre-Revolutionary house, built of wide, hand-hewn boards. The downstairs had once been the stable, the upstairs the servant's quarters for a tavern, now a lovely old stone house that stood on the corner of the road next door to Woodhill. A quarter of a mile away, facing the brow of Jericho Mountain, was Headquarter's Farm. It had been bought by our old family friend Edith Mellor. George Washington lived there prior to the battle of Trenton. He made occasional visits to the local tavern, and he slept in Edith's house. At least his horse had slept in ours.

Meanwhile, Dad and Maggie, who had been living in Laguna Beach, hopped on a freighter to go around the world, but one look at Tahiti and they abandoned ship. They settled on the island of Morea in a grass hut next to the lagoon where Dad's paintings got better, just like Gauguin's. They would have stayed forever, if Dad hadn't fallen prey to that discomforting malady that so often afflicts travelers in the unspoiled tropics. I was left with no home base in California, so I hitched a ride across the country with a group fellow students, one of whom owned a car.

I had hoped to get a job in New Hope for the summer and earn some money, but Mum explained that she had to go back to England. Grandad had died at the house of his mistress, Mabel. Until then I hadn't known he had one. Uncle Jack had been dispatched to fetch the body. "It was all very embarrassing," said Mum. She wanted to console Gran, who knew all about Mabel and loved Grandad no matter what. She told me, "I've been counting on you to keep house, cook, and take care of Bill (my twelve-year-old half-brother) while I'm gone."

The garden of Woodhill was a rough acre of grass on the edge of a cornfield. Mum and Geoff had done their best with it. They'd started to build a terrace and a rock garden. They'd had a neighboring farmer plow up half the lawn behind the open-fronted carriage house that

Ruth B. Morris
Eagle Road
Newtown, R. D. 2, Pa.

clean. & they can be sat on without showing
the dirt.

Geoff does his bookwork up there —
Bill his home work. & I my sewing
ironing & mending. mostly due to
the size of the room. & being able to
leave one back indidily if not
complete.   Also our living quarters
have been very cramped in the white
house due to having no living room —
we started in the laundry. but it
always looked so messy — we migrated
to your room.

I'm not procrastinating about your job
but branch people will be more in the
mood for thinking about their summer
help problems — I'm sure I could do
so good now.

Much love from all of us — & get
some sleep —   Mmm —
  P.S. It was 70° last Thursday & the white
Jasmine & Japonica are out, I mean blooming
in the garden. And today they are coated in
ice — after a bad ice storm. They look

OPPOSITE Letter from Mum during my freshman year in college with a P.S. about the garden. As it turned out, there was no summer job. Grandad died, Mum went to England; and I kept house.

ABOVE Woodhill, the house in Bucks County where I saw the gnome. In the background just to the right of the multitrunked ornamental cherry tree on the left are the steps on which Mr. Brown and I sat while watching the fireflies. In this photo Mum and Geoff have already completed a flagstone terrace and built a small but charming rock garden beneath it. Rock gardens gained popularity in Pennsylvania in the forties and succeeded far better than herbaceous borders.

TOP A map I made as a Christmas card in 1950.

Geoff used for a garage, and here they'd planted a big vegetable garden. They'd also made an oval island bed in the lawn and filled it with zinnias to provide cut flowers for the house. The problem was every night some mystery animal was smashing them down.

Mum had worked all winter painting walls and making curtains out of sheets. She could turn an ordinary house into a palace on a shoestring and do it so quickly it made your head spin. She and Geoff had also found a dog, a large, honey-colored, smooth-haired mongrel called Mr. Brown. Part boxer, he had a smiling face and was one of those great dogs one remembers all one's life.

"You can get fresh milk from the next farm down the road," Mum told me, "and Edith Mellor has built a swimming pool. You can ride her horses if you can catch them. Our new friends Gert and Henry Bristol are enormously kind and live less than a mile away. They have an older horse, easier to catch but duller to ride." The friendship with the Bristols had begun when Henry passed our house on his way home from the New York-Trenton train. He noticed Mum up on a ladder painting the house and stopped to chat. The next day he brought her a basketful of the best paint brushes money could buy. This unassuming man in old clothes was the president of Bristol Myers.

Before the end of July, Mum had sailed for England. Geoff stayed in New York all week where he had an apartment and a studio. He came home only on the weekends. Bill went to summer school at Newtown Friends and had to go to bed early, so weeknights I was glad to have good books to read and Mr. Brown for company. On one of those first nights after Mum had left and Bill had gone to bed, I sat on the back steps with Mr. Brown beside me. I watched the evening light fade from the western sky until the stars began to twinkle behind the corn field at the back of the garden and fireflies began to rise out of the lawn.

Back in the house I curled up with a book in a comfortable wing chair next to the empty fireplace, and Mr. Brown stretched out at my feet. After about an hour he pricked up his ears, looked at me strangely, and started to whine. "What's the matter, fella?" I asked. As if in answer, he ran to the kitchen door, then back toward me grinning and wagging from tip to toe. It occurred to me that whatever animal had been smashing down the zinnias might be at it again, so I clipped Mr. Brown's leash onto his collar. Then, holding the leash tightly with one hand and a flashlight in the other I stepped warily outdoors. Mr. Brown shot out the door. He pulled me headlong down the steps and dragged me across the lawn now wet with dew. I hung onto his leash for dear life as we zoomed straight past the zinnias in the direction of the empty coach house that Mum and Geoff used for a garage.

When Mr. Brown reached the open front of the old coach house, he stopped dead in his tracks, and I almost fell over him. Then he crouched down and started to bark. I shone the flashlight against the back wall, and my heart began to pound slowly and hard. I felt every beat. I could hardly believe what my eyes saw, but I did indeed see it. Caught in the circle cast by my flashlight stood what appeared to be a real live gnome, about eighteen inches tall. He stood bolt upright with his back against the wall, his elbows bent, and his little hands close to his chest. He had two bright gleaming eyes, a round shiny nose, pointed ears, a black face and hands and a white beard. The most incredible thing of all was that on his little round head he wore a tall pointed cap. "A gnome!" I thought. "So gnomes really do exist, but why am I afraid?" I hung onto Mr. Brown's leash with all my might.

This gnome of mine looked exactly like an Irish leprechaun except for one important detail. Instead of wearing green like all the Little People I'd ever heard of, my gnome was wearing evening dress. On his chest he sported a spotless white shirt neatly tucked into little black pants, his plump arms were clothed in a handsome black jacket, his pointed ears were exactly the shape of a gnome's ears—though in this case they were black—and his lovely pointed cap was edged crisply in white to match his tuxedo. Never taking his eyes off us, he sidled from corner to corner of the coachhouse. Then, realizing he was trapped, suddenly my cute little gnome changed. He dropped to all fours and whirled about so we could see him from the side. In an instant, he turned himself into a skunk! What I'd taken for a pointed cap was actually the tip of a skunk's striped tail held aloft behind him.

I let out a yelp, grabbed Mr. Brown by the collar, and the two of us raced out of there like a couple of antelopes. I'd seen the front of that skunk and had no desire to see his rear. We dashed back across the lawn and leaped the steps into the house. Once safely inside, I got the giggles, collapsed on the floor, and threw my arms around Mr. Brown. He covered my face with wet kisses. And then I turned sober. For a moment I'd been right back there with the ancient Celts. To this day I keep the statue of a gnome in my garden to remind me of that time long ago when I too saw Puck one midsummer night. And I was not dreaming.

5.

Romancing the Compost Pile

"Behold this compost! behold it well!

What chemistry!

Earth grows such sweet things out of such corruptions."

"This Compost," Walt Whitman, 1867

THE IDEA OF digging fragrant, black, crumbly compost out of your very own compost pile is dear to the heart of every gardener. It didn't surprise me the other day when a neighbor stopped me on the street and without preamble asked, "Do you have a compost pile?" Nor, after I'd replied that I wouldn't be without one, did it astonish me that she asked if she and her husband could drop by to see it. They haven't shown up yet for the scenic tour, but some of my neighbor's questions have set me thinking. With composting you can fluff up your soil and fill it with billions of health-giving microorganisms. Break the rules and you can end up with a public nuisance.

There are only two basic ways to make compost, the slow or cold way and the rapid or hot way. All the methods you hear about are simply variations on these two major themes. Rapid hot composting requires the right ingredients, a certain amount of technical know-how, and a lot of hard work to toss and turn the pile—we'll get to all that in due time. But slow, cold composting can be as simple as Mr. McGregor's rubbish heap in Beatrice Potter's stories about Peter Rabbit. You may remember that Mr. McGregor dumped all his garden waste over the wall that stood at the back of his garden. Logic leads us to believe it slowly decomposed. In *The Flopsy Bunnies* we're shown a picture of it, a messy looking affair with mountains of chopped grass, a rotten vegetable marrow, several jam pots, some paper bags, and an old boot or two.

"One day—oh joy!—" we're told, "there were a quantity of overgrown lettuces which had 'shot' into flower." These we can assume would soon break down along with the vegetable marrow and add their decayed remains to the pile (if not first consumed by the Flopsy Bunnies). Doubtless the frequent soft rains and cold winters of England's Lake District helped speed the decomposition of every organic thing that landed on the pile. But Mr. McGregor's rubbish heap was a far cry from a well organized, properly constructed compost pile. It attracted mice. We're even intro-duced to one by name—"Thomasina Tittlemouse, a woodmouse with a long tail." And flies! ("Blue bottles.") Benjamin Bunny avoided them by putting his head in a paper sack. Obviously, this kind of happy-go-lucky rubbish heap would never do today, except in rural areas.

At Hoyle Court the rubbish heap was hidden behind a retaining wall at the back of the vegetable garden, just like Mr. McGregor's. All Viney, the gardener, had to do was wheel his barrow full of garden trash to the edge of the wall and tip it out. But Viney's rubbish heap was more refined than Mr. McGregor's. No jam pots, paper bags, or old boots. It was only a step or two removed from a proper compost pile. From time to time, Viney trun-dled an empty wheelbarrow out the back gate and down the slope to the rubbish heap with John running down the path in front of him and me skipping along behind. Once there, Viney dug out a load of finished com-post from the bottom of the heap. A large portion of the finished black stuff had been sliced off, and the rest was held back with posts and planks.

Once Viney had filled his barrow to overflowing, he puffed his way back up the path, through the garden, and into the potting shed. There, in the dim light of the shed from beneath the patient man's elbow or some other spot equally under foot, we watched him sieve the precious stuff, mix it with an equal portion of good garden loam, and put the resulting mix into flats and pots for planting seeds and cuttings. John kept up a barrage of questions. For once I was silent. With my nose slightly above bench height, I breathed in the magical odor of sweet moist compost and understood without words that it was both the end and the beginning of all growing things.

As soon as Geoff married Mum and moved into Chess Cottage, he started a garden dump on the other side of the wattle fence at the back of the garden, but instead of calling it a rubbish heap he gave it the more elegant name of compost pile. One minute he'd wax romantic about Mum, chasing her through the shrubbery and spouting his special lingo, a cross between Biblical and Shakespearean English and French slang. The next minute he'd be moony over his beloved compost.

"Now harken, GOSSE, unto thy elder!" Geoff would intone, brandishing his pitchfork over John's and my heads and addressing us jointly, as he always did, with the French word for brats. "Regular additions of YUMMY compost can turn thin, humus-poor soils into the dark-brown, rich, productive stuff all GREAT gardeners yearn for!" To this day I save all our fruit and vegetable peelings for the compost pile. It really bothers me if for any reason I can't run outdoors and down the garden path with drippy little offerings to the temple of divine rot.

One reason these old-fashioned cold compost piles worked as well as they did is that, beyond the occasional thick woody stalk of cabbage or brussels sprouts, they didn't contain a large proportion of woody material. Those were the days before the passage of anti-burning laws, when every suburban or country household had a burning pile. People burned all their combustible garden trash—fallen leaves, twigs, branches, and large woody hedge clippings, plus all the waste paper and cardboard from the house. Great fun for the children. At Rickmansworth, in company with my best friend Elizabeth Wrigley and her brothers, I learned the joy of digging up forbidden potatoes from Mrs. Wrigley's kitchen garden and roasting them in the burning pile that was forever smoldering away at the bottom of the garden. Ah, the smoky aroma and magic earthy taste (with unmistakable hints of scorched wet newspaper) of those half-cooked, stolen marvels!

In Hollywood as late as 1945, my family along with everyone else in our neighborhood had a small concrete incinerator in the backyard and a sheet of instructions telling us on which days to burn. That was my job and I enjoyed it. For several years after Lou and I moved to Del Mar, I also burned all our eucalyptus leaves in a perfectly legal pile with a ring of rocks around it. But eventually, people realized that it wasn't a good idea to pump the atmosphere full of carbon dioxide, to say nothing of the danger of fire. I turned my former burning ring into a flower bed, and the potassium-rich earth in it grew the best and biggest cinerarias—three feet tall and equally wide—I've ever seen. Wood ashes are a strong source of potassium, but they're also highly alkaline, so don't use them on heavy clay soils that are alkaline and fail to leach out quickly.

Soon, power-driven chippers roared on the scene. If you can stand the din, a good chipper can reduce a huge pile of brush into a small pile of mulch in short order. It can also grind up a mountain of spent vegetables and flowers to fit nicely into the compost pile. And here's where hot composting comes in, because it works so rapidly. A hot compost pile can give you a usable product within two or three weeks. Furthermore, a hot compost pile kills most weed seeds and all insects, insect eggs, and most plant disease-producing organisms. (Heat-resistant viruses such as tobacco mosaic virus will survive.)

Slow or cool-composting can sometimes take as long as six months or maybe even a year to get a usable product. Also, it doesn't kill weed seeds and may or may not kill pests and plant diseases. (Some are smothered during the rotting process, but the end product isn't pasteurized by heat as in the hot method.) On the other hand, compost made the slow way retains more of the desirable microbes that help your plants resist disease. Either way, I feel I'm doing something for the environment and for my garden soil. All compost contains billions of health-giving microorganisms in every handful.

My present compost pile is concealed behind a gate at the very bottom of the garden just over the fence from a small cozy patio where Lou and I have lunch on most sunny days all winter long. For years I made compost here by the slow method, in pits about a foot deep and four-feet square. Pit composting makes sense in dry climates, since it's easier to keep the pile damp. In wet weather, you throw a tarp over it to keep

PHOTO BY MELINDA HOLDEN

EVERY SUNNY DAY in winter Lou and I lunch outdoors in the protected patio at the bottom of the garden. Just beyond the fence behind Lou is the compost pile.

the pit from filling with water. Some gardeners will tell you this will also keep off flies, but, believe me, it doesn't. Instead, when you add kitchen leavings to an existing pile it's best to cover them over either with finished compost or a bit of earth. (Earth makes compost heavy. It should never be used in a hot compost pile.)

All went well until roots from vines, shrubs, and trees invaded the pit. I had nowhere to move it, so I decided to take the plunge and invest in a set of compost bins, floored with a sheet of plywood. Bins are the best way to make hot compost. They save space, hold the pile in shape, retain heat, and let in air. My set-up fills a nine-by-five-foot area. It consists of three, open-topped bins, each measuring three feet in height and width by five feet in depth. (Three-feet square is the ideal size for a compost pile.) Their frame is sturdy redwood, and they're lined with one-quarter inch hardware cloth. Each bin has a removable front wall consisting of planks that slide down into grooves. You can slide them into place as you build a new pile and then slide them out again to dig out the compost or toss it into the next bin. Lou calls my compost bins "Pat's Folly." I have to admit it will take me a month of compost spreading to make them pay for themselves. They cost me $500. (Don't faint! You could construct a similar set for a lot less, if you don't hire a carpenter or use redwood, both of which I did.)

As soon as the stain was dry I built my first hot compost pile in the first bin. The method is technical, so skip over it if you couldn't care less. But if you're still with me, you start by spreading a three-to-four inch thick layer of carbonaceous matter on the bottom of the pile. Stack an equally sized layer of nitrogenous material on top of that. Carbonaceous wastes are drier materials like dry leaves, spent plants, hay, corn stalks, sawdust, or dry grass clippings. Nitrogenous materials are usually wet or soft green wastes like fruit and vegetable scraps, fresh grass clippings, lettuce leaves, flower petals, soft green leaves, and fresh manure. Before adding the materials to your compost pile, chop them up into particles about one-half to one and one-half inches in size. My system is to lay leafy material on top of the pile and whack them into pieces with a sharp machete.

Continue stacking alternate layers until you've built a pile approximately three feet tall. If you think you're a bit light on nitrogenous wastes, sprinkle some sulfate of ammonia, a strong source of nitrogen, on top of the carbonaceous layers as you build them up. Dampen the whole thing down with water from the hose, so that the materials are moist but not soggy. (A piece of plastic tucked loosely over the top of the bin can help hold in heat and moisture and keep off rain, or cover the bins with corrugated roofing.) When your pile heats up, toss the material into the second bin, putting the outside parts in the center and the inside parts to the outside. Then toss the compost back and forth between the second and third bins every day or two until it's finished. Meanwhile, start a new pile in the first bin.

If you have the right mix of ingredients the pile will heat up to 160 degrees Fahrenheit within twenty-four to forty-eight hours. Some mail-order garden catalogs offer special thermometers for measuring the temperature inside a compost pile, but if you've got a hot pile it steams and you know it. That's the cue to begin tossing. Once hot compost has started working, it's best not to add additional organic materials. During this period, I add my kitchen leavings straight into my garden soil as sheet compost. To do this, simply dig a hole about a spade-blade deep between vegetables or flowers, pour in the chopped fruit and vegetable scraps, sprinkle a couple of tablespoons of fertilizer and a trowelful of chicken manure on top, and cover with about eight inches of soil. Wet kitchen peelings decompose quickly, releasing nitrogen straight into the soil. In a month or two, you can dig into the spot and instead of a wet mass of smelly garbage, you'll find soft black earth and plenty of earthworms.

Tossing and turning a compost pile regularly mixes air into the compost. Air adds the necessary oxygen, and it also cools down the mixture so it stays at the optimum temperature and keeps the decomposition process going. If you don't toss and turn a compost pile, it will get so hot inside that the beneficial microorganisms will be killed and the pile will cool down before the composting process is complete. Mismanaged compost piles have been known to burst into flames. As the compost cooks, it will gradually change texture and reduce in size. Once it cools down and has a soft spongy texture, a sweet earthy smell, and a rich dark color, it's ready to use. You can take out any remaining lumps and add them to the next batch.

Here are a few rules that apply to all compost piles, hot or cold. Don't ever add meat, bones, sauces, or fat, since these attract rats. Don't add droppings of dogs, cats, lions, or other meat-eating animals, since these can carry dangerous disease organisms. Don't add dead fish because they create unpleasant odors that attract both flies and cats. Garden soil should never be added to hot compost; it cools down the pile and makes the compost too heavy to toss and turn. Don't add lime or limestone to a compost pile; it causes a chemical reaction that creates ammonia gas, which in turn wastes nitrogen.

A word of warning about fresh grass clippings. These are an excellent source of nitrogen. It saddens me to see them bagged and sent to the dump, but unless grass is broken up and separated by dryer materials it tends to stick together into a solid, wet, leathery mat that won't properly decompose. If you have a lot of grass clippings, you can use an alternative method. Construct the entire pile out of a mixture of fresh grass with dry leaves—the ratio is three parts leaves to one grass. A mixture of dry hay and fresh grass mixed in roughly even proportions is particularly excellent since it composts easily. Eucalyptus leaves contain an oil that makes them slow to decompose, but even they'll break down eventually. Compost made from them doesn't kill plants.

If your compost pile contains too much nitrogenous waste it will smell of ammonia. Fix it by sprinkling a few handfuls of wood shavings or saw-dust into the pile as you toss it or simply by adding a little of it to the part of the pile that smells. If your pile is too light on nitrogen you'll know it because it won't heat up properly; you can correct this by mixing in more nitrogen in the form of sulfate of ammonia or other nitrogenous materi-als like grass clippings, fresh chicken manure, or urine diluted with five parts of water. A pile that's too wet will fail to heat up, but don't let a pile dry out or it will stop cooking. Add water if necessary to keep it damp.

A properly made compost pile smells good as it works—a little like mushrooms—so there's no need to worry about odor. You may also notice white mold forming on the outside; it's natural and nothing to worry about. Flies or other insects are sometimes attracted to hot com-post as it steams, but they can't breed in it because the heat kills their eggs and larvae. A piece of plastic loosely laid over a hot compost pile really does help to discourage insects since it holds in the steam.

And don't forget that if hot composting sounds like too much work, you can always settle for the easier way. For more years than I care to count, I made compost in those messy heaps of organic materials that moldered away in happy isolation, until I thought they'd decomposed enough to be safely added to the garden. Some of my compost piles got hot for a while and others stayed cold. Other than adding the stuff from the kitchen and keeping the whole thing damp I mainly forgot about it. Eventually, I stopped adding to a pile and let it sit. After a few months, I would dig deeply into it to find gorgeous black, sweet smelling organic matter like something out of the north woods. And every finished forkful wriggled with earthworms. By whatever method I make my compost, the fragrance of it has the power to waft me to another time and place. Viney's strong Yorkshire accent rings in my ears, and once again I'm standing with my nose just above the bench inside his potting shed.

6.

The Toad Who Knew His Way Home

FOR MANY YEARS I've attempted to live in harmony with a few garden pests without allowing the landscape to look like a chewed-up disaster. One way to accomplish this is to confuse harmful insects and arachnids by growing a wide variety of plants and mixing them up. For example, instead of arranging your herbs in a knot or a circle and lining up your roses like gawky chorus girls with long prickly legs, place them hither and yon wherever they look best. This muddles the pests, because they find it harder to specialize on one favored plant. It may sound funny, but it works. And the garden looks all the prettier for it.

Equally important is crop rotation, the practice of moving annual plants around from year to year, so you're not growing a particular crop (or in some cases a flower) in the same place for two years in succession. Ideally, you should wait three years before planting an annual in the same spot again. This applies to all vegetables but especially to tomatoes, cucumbers, cabbage crops, lettuces, and onions, and, among flowers, to stock, ranunculus, and larkspur. Crop rotation prevents a build-up of pests and diseases common to each plant. It also slows the depletion of nutrients in the soil, since some crops such as corn take lots of nitrogen out of soil while legumes such as peas and beans add it back.

Practicing good garden hygiene is another prime step toward a healthy garden—cutting off diseased leaves or flowers instead of letting them fall onto the ground—as is fertilizing properly and providing good drainage and productive soil. Bugs make a beeline for unhealthy plants. Of course, one always wants to choose pest- and disease-resistant varieties—tomatoes with VFN after their name (meaning they're resistant to verticillium and fusarium wilts and nematodes), for example, and Lady Banks roses that never get mildew, rust, aphids, or caterpillars.

One can practice these passive techniques meticulously and still need an active system of defense in case of attack. For me, this system is Integrated Pest Management (IPM). Mainly this means cooperating with nature by releasing beneficial organisms and taking care not to kill such visible helpmates as spiders, small wasps, hover flies, dragonflies, frogs, toads, lizards, or the nearly invisible larval forms of beneficial insects and arachnids that are part of the natural makeup of the garden. It's like having an army of diminutive palace guards patrolling your property night and day. Some stand at attention in guard houses, some burrow under the ground, some march to and fro on top of it, and still others patrol the air. IPM is also a strategy of spraying seldom and then only when absolutely necessary. When you do spray, choose specific sprays against specific pests, and avoid broad-spectrum sprays that kill a wide variety of pests but also kill great quantities of beneficials.

Forty years ago, I was much less sure of the right path to take in pest control. Prior to the 1960s, most gardeners thought that regular spraying with pesticides, especially malathion, was the only way to go. Chlordane, now a proven carcinogen, was an accepted ground spray against termites, ants, and beetles. Worse still, a great many gardeners of the late fifties and early sixties sprayed the whole garden with DDT once a year—in dry climates that's all it took—to control caterpillars and ants. People were unaware of the immense hazard it posed to birds and other wildlife, not to mention humans. On one occasion, I used it too.

Deep in my heart, I didn't believe in using dangerous chemicals, but also I detested spraying. I still do. If you've ever dolled yourself up in mask, showercap, and boots until you resemble a creature from outer space and then tried to undo bottles, grasp spoons, and measure out exact quantities of sloppy liquids while wearing a pair of rubber gloves and goggles that continually steam over, you'll understand.

I knew people who coped with spraying much better than I. One of them was Mum's third and last husband, Bill Begley, a charming, good-looking Pennsylvania lawyer with an Irish wit and an English passion for gardening. In 1951 Mum had flown out to California for Lou's and my wedding and though she returned to Pennsylvania, she never went home to Woodhill. Geoff's alcoholism had increased, and now he was threatening to return to England. For Mum this was the last straw. So, after eighteen years of unhappiness and insecurity with Geoff, she divorced him. A year or two later she met and married Bill, who was five years her junior. It was a happy marriage. When Bill retired, they moved to California to be close to John and me and our growing families. But for the first ten years of their marriage, Mum and Bill lived in a handsome stone house that he had built on the banks of the Delaware River. It had a guesthouse and five acres of woods and gardens. Lou and I and our daughters, Francie and Wendy, spent our summer vacations there. John and his first wife, Lore, who died many years ago, and their three wonderful sons, Jordan, Jeremy, and Jotham, did the same.

Bill Begley kept us laughing. Everyone, including Dad and Maggie, was fond of him; our children adored him. Mum credited Bill's upright character and geniality to the first five years of his life when he'd basked in the affection of fifty jolly Irish nuns. When he was just a toddler, his father had died. His mother couldn't cope, so she sent Bill and his older brother to a Catholic boarding school. Since Bill was so young, the nuns decided he should live with them inside the convent, where he soon became the center of attention. He grew up with all the social graces, played a good game of bridge, and was a fine golfer. But among his many talents, Bill's ability to insert humor into everyday life and conversation was the one that most endeared him to his family and friends. When Francie and Wendy were children and our car turned into the Begleys' drive, they'd often start to giggle in anticipation before Lou had set the brake. Then they'd leap out and run straight to Bill. "Thank you," he said to me once, "for giving me the children and grandchildren I never had."

We also loved Bill's and Mum's Pennsylvania garden, which featured a large lawn surrounding a swimming pool, a rock garden bordering the woods, shady paths edged with azaleas, and a Japanese garden they'd built after spending a month in Japan. But though Bill was an avid plantsman, he was cut from a different patch of turf than Geoff. Bill was not an organic gardener; far from it. Once a week wherever he and Mum lived—either in Pennsylvania or California—he sprayed malathion on everything in his garden until nothing buzzed, not even a bee. Whenever I left his spotless environs and went home to confront my chewed-up plants I felt pangs of guilt. It appeared to me that he was the conscientious gardener and I was the lazy one.

I even remember having seen my first stepfather, that ultimate organic gardener Geoffrey Morris, sprayer in hand, looking as though he positively relished the Battle of the Bug. He didn't just sit there and let his plants get eaten alive like I did. But shortly after his divorce from Mum, Geoff moved back to England, married a young aristocratic lawyer named Jenny, and enrolled my half-brother Bill in an English school.

Although I still wrote to Geoff about gardening, photography, and painting and enjoyed his energetic replies, filled with advice in Elizabethan English and peppered with capital letters, exclamation marks, and French, I hadn't yet broached the topic of garden sprays.

Then one day Mother Nature took a hand in my education. Her message was loud and clear, and the messenger she chose was none other than a common garden toad. A few days previously, I'd discovered this lovely fat toad living beneath a rock near a waterfall I'd built outside our kitchen window. Good gardeners everywhere treasure toads. They eat great quantities of pests—everything from grasshoppers, earwigs, ants, moths, and beetles, including bitter-tasting cucumber beetles, to sowbugs, flies, centipedes, and slugs. And they don't just eat a few of these creatures; they stuff on them.

That lovely morning near the end of April, I awoke early, having made up my mind to spray my Algerian ivy with DDT because it was being decimated by caterpillars. I planned to don a mask and protective clothing, cover my birdbath and waterfall with sheets of plastic, and protect my toad by reestablishing him in the garden of my in-laws, Frances and John Lloyd Wright, who lived next door to us but higher on the hill. (John was Frances's third husband and the second son of Frank Lloyd Wright.)

I'd read that toads will settle down in your garden if you make them a house out of an upside-down pot with a rock on top, to cover the drainage hole, and a hole broken in the rim to serve as a door. I found a pot that filled the bill and hid it on the edge of the Wrights' patio in a damp mossy spot near their waterfall. Then I donned gloves, caught the toad, and carried him up the path that wound up the hill by means of steps, stepping stones, and brick walkways. It was an attractive path with other paths branching off it, but not easy to negotiate.

Having placed the toad safely in his new home, I went back down

FOR TWENTY-EIGHT years Lou's mother, Frances, and her husband, John Lloyd Wright, lived next door to us in this house. After they died, we sold it to the parents of one of our sons-in-law. Beyond the Mediterranean fan palm is the path my toad took home.

ABOUT 30 YEARS AGO I built this waterfall out of rocks and concrete. My toad lived beneath it.

the path to our house and sprayed the ivy. When the job was finished and I'd washed up, I ran across the lawn again to check on him. At the end of our property there was, and still is, a flight of steps I'd made by arranging sacks of ready-made concrete on the slope, turning the hose onto them, and tearing off the paper after the concrete had hardened. When I reached this spot, an amazing sight stopped me dead in my tracks: Jumping resolutely down those steps was my fat little toad. I lunged forward and caught him in mid air. No, I didn't get warts, and I didn't kiss him either. (Toads don't turn into princes, only frogs; anyway, I already had a prince.)

Never have I heard that toads, like carrier pigeons, are gifted with a homing instinct, but this one was. Hop by hop he'd traveled down that winding path and found his way home. I put my homing toad into a cardboard carton and supplied him with food and water. Then, chastened, I rinsed off the area surrounding our waterfall. In the evening after the ground had dried I replaced the toad in his hole. He backed himself quickly into it and seemed content. First thing in the morning I peered beneath the rock. The toad was gone. It was only then that I realized the full impact of what I'd done; I'd killed off my toad's food supply and that of any other beneficial creature who might have been living in my garden.

Never again did I spray with DDT, but the lesson went even deeper. At last I understood what I should have known all along; if you want beneficial creatures to set up housekeeping in your garden you've got to have a enough pests for them to eat. When Rachel Carson wrote her celebrated book *Silent Spring,* alerting the public to the danger inherent in the irresponsible use of pesticides, especially DDT, I enthusiastically embraced her philosophy. It was such a relief to stop feeling guilty. People's attitudes changed overnight. At last I could point with pride at my wild garden with its worm-eaten leaves. But help was on the way because the crusade begun by Rachel Carson was carried on by others. First came BT (*Bacillus thuringiensis,* a bacteria that kills certain leaf-eating caterpillars but nothing else), followed by a host of other environmentally responsible sprays. Then the Department of Agriculture, the Agricultural Extension, and private industry began to explore ways to increase the numbers of beneficial organisms that naturally abound in our gardens.

Now there's a continual hunt going on in many parts of the world to find beneficial organisms that are the natural enemies of some of our worst pests; once found, they are raised and released. Among beneficials that can be purchased from commercial sources today are ladybugs, praying mantises, several nematodes, various types of predatory mites, green lacewings, syrphid flies, and many types of wasps, including whitefly parasites (*Encarsia formosa*), and trichogramma wasps that lay their eggs on caterpillars. If we release enough of these creatures and provide them with an appropriate environment, we really can live in complete harmony with pests without ever having to spray.

In my garden I've found that simply releasing several packages of ladybugs beginning in early spring and continuing throughout the growing months reduces pest problems to such an extent that spraying is usually unnecessary. It's not the adult ladybug that kills the pests but the immature larval stage of the insect. The same is true of lacewings. Although ladybugs are sold mainly as a control for aphids, it's been my experience that they may also control immature stages of whiteflies and mites, including fuchsia gall mites.

Perhaps the fact that I have a large garden with a dense shrubbery around it and many different plants mixed up together helps the ladybugs settle down long enough to lay a few eggs. I have a special method for letting them loose in the landscape. Approximately one hour before sunset, I put the package containing the ladybugs into the refrigerator.

This slows their metabolism and makes them less likely to fly away. Meanwhile, I lightly mist the foliage of the plants in the garden—ladybugs need moisture. At dusk I take the package of ladybugs out of the refrigerator and deposit little spoonfuls of the groggy beetles here and there around the garden. Evening hours make ladybugs sleepy; by morning they may have settled down and decided to stay.

I've also released lacewings, reputed to be a first-rate control. They're less migratory than ladybugs. I've applied beneficial nematodes to the soil. They seem to have reduced the number of root knot nematodes, cutworms, and white grubs. On several occasions, I've placed the egg sacks of praying mantises in my garden. My praying mantises enthusiastically ate each other, but they also ate a lot of pests. Many beneficials have moved in uninvited and set up housekeeping in my garden. At this very moment one of them is close at hand, policing my garden and keeping pests at bay. Just now, I glanced outdoors and saw a hover fly settling here and there on the gamolepis blossoms outside my window.

There are plenty of lizards in my garden, including alligator lizards—those that aren't squashed by cars when they foolishly sun themselves down on the road. Tree frogs are also native here and help to keep mosquitoes at bay. Spiders abound in my garden. If it were not for them, pests would have destroyed all vegetation on this planet eons ago. Mail-order outlets sell special gadgets for catching spiders alive. I have one of these, but I also use damp cosmetic tissues, which I drop over them and then gently close beneath. The spider crawls up inside, and I take it outside and deposit it on a hanging basket fuchsia. Soon each of my fuchsias has a resident spider sitting on top, happily consuming the various pests that favor fuchsias. I never need spray my fuchsias. By midsummer, you can see slight damage from rust mite but never enough to bother about.

Birds, too, can be a help in controlling caterpillars and many other

MY SUMMER 1993 vegetable garden, edged with "Perfection Orange" hybrid African marigolds, was particularly productive. Here's one day's harvest. At the end of the season, all the "dead bodies" of the old plants get recycled into compost. So do the peelings from the vegetables.

pests. One reason I grow many informal shrubs, along with tall trees, around the outer perimeter of our garden is to encourage them. We also have a lotus bowl, a bird bath, and a little waterfall for them. For years we had a pet scrub jay—Peanut Boy—who came right into the children's playbay, an area that connected their bedrooms and had a Dutch door that opened onto the garden. Now one of these garrulous birds joins Lou and me for lunch every day in the winter patio. He comes to our hands for peanuts and perches on our knees. Mainly he sits on the rose arbor eyeing the garden fiercely and darting down for caterpillars. Mockingbirds and other song birds catch flying insects, mites, and beetles in the trees. Even hummingbirds catch tiny insects.

At one time we had bats that rid us of millions of night-flying moths—the ones that breed budworms. Alas, no longer; the backcountry is filled with houses, and the bats' habitat is destroyed. A few owls are still here to catch mice and rats. I can hear them at night softly hooting, a sound that always makes me happy. Gardeners who have large trees and are into conservation can encourage both these beneficial creatures by installing houses for them.

Working with beneficials and putting up with a few blemishes is an easier way to garden than constant spraying, and it makes you feel good. The garden is, after all, a microcosm of nature. Continual conflict is going on, but somehow it's all harmonious. The unseen battles are all there right under our noses—wasp against caterpillar, spider against mite, and bug against bug—but the less we humans mix in and destroy their balance the better. I like to walk out into my garden and know it's a living place, not a dead one. I love to hear the buzzing of bees at midday, the chirping of frogs in the evening, and mockingbirds singing all night just as beautifully as English nightingales. Then I feel the harmony of nature can be almost as real in a garden as it is in the wild. All we have to do is give it a place to abide.

ORNAMENTAL GARDENING

7.

The Wisteria That Wouldn't Give Up

I T W A S Y E A R S since I'd visited Hampton Court, Henry VIII's country house ten miles up the Thames from London, and Lou had never been there. When my cousins David and Doreen suggested an outing especially to see the gardens, we were delighted to accept their invitation. We visited the incredible maze, enjoyed Anne Bolyn's garden at the height of bloom, and admired the tree roses planted in green-hedged sunken beds so one could look down on the flowers from above. Then David asked if we'd like to see the oldest vine in England.

"It's in a greenhouse just beyond the roses."

"Love to," I answered, "but what kind of vine is it?"

"I'm not sure whether it's red or white. Probably red, wouldn't you think, Doreen? We'll ask."

"Not what color. I mean what kind of plant is it? Ivy? Wisteria? Virginia creeper?"

"But a vine is a vine, is it not?" asked David, fixing me with his noble eye. (David is the eleventh Lord Strabolgi, a Scottish title that goes back to the Middle Ages, and he sits in the House of Lords.) "Naturally, Pat, it has to be a grape. Just think of the words vineyard, vintner, vin, or wine. What else could a vine be? All those other plants are called climbers."

David's reasoning was indisputable, but whether climbing plants are known as vines as they are in America or climbers as they are in England, no garden is complete without a few of those flexuous plants that either trail on the ground or climb up a support. Vines add grace and charm to the landscape. They soften harsh lines, cover bare ground and lend character to buildings. It's always seemed to me that vines must have twined their way particularly closely into the psyche of mankind. Bacchus had something to do with it, but long before wine was invented people must have felt a natural kinship with a plant that could embrace another. My own first memory is of a vine. I recall waking up in my pram, one of those commodious English baby carriages, and gazing with delight at a wall overgrown with Virginia creeper. This leafy paradise was alive with hundreds of birds. They'd built their nests among its leaves and branches, and they filled the air with song. What a beautiful world I'd awakened into! The green face of nature smiled down on me, and I smiled back.

Among all vines, one in particular has wound itself most prominently into my heart, my garden, and my life. That vine is the wisteria. When I was eighteen years old, I was captivated by a purple wisteria. It was because of this particular wisteria that I coveted a second-story room on a southeast corner of my college dorm. The room had its drawbacks. It faced south so it was hot in summer; it was at the head of the stairs, so it was often noisy, but like many people with glaring flaws in their characters, it also had great charm. Its chief boast was a pair of French doors that could be flung open wide onto a private balcony. Below the balcony was a quiet and secluded patio in which grew a venerable wisteria. This wisteria had climbed a drain pipe, then a beam, stretched along a section of red tile roof, caught hold of the corner of the balcony, and twined all over its wrought-iron railings.

The first time I saw that wisteria burst into bloom was in April of my freshman year at Scripps. I stood on the patio below the blossom-covered balcony, delirious with spring and drunk with the heady perfume of cascading purple blooms. I

TOLL HALL AT Scripps. Beyond the palm trees (center) the French doors of my upstairs room and balcony, once covered with wisteria, can be glimpsed.

put my name in for the room at the head of the stairs so when I became an upper classman it would be mine. For two years I waited, and meanwhile I sometimes visualized myself studying on my peaceful balcony, surrounded by the wisteria's bare twisted limbs in winter, its fragrant purple blooms in spring, and shaded by its cool green leaves in summer.

Before my junior year, my brother John, who was studying architecture at Berkeley, and I both worked at odd jobs and tutoring to save enough money to go back to England and spend the summer with Uncle Jack. That was the summer of 1949, ten years after we'd emigrated to America and one year after Grandad's death. Gran and Uncle Jack and one or two aged servants were still living at Hoyle Court. Neglected during the war, the gardens now had a poetic, almost ghostly beauty. Viney was now the only gardener and spent most of his time growing fruit and vegetables to sell in the village. but he still found time to raise flowers for the house. When I entered my old bedroom, there standing on a chest in front of the open window was one of Viney's huge romantic

TELEPHONES
BRADFORD. 28456. 7. 8. 9.

CODE A B C. 5TH EDITION.

TELEGRAMS:
"AMBLER, BRADFORD"

ESTABLISHED · 1789.

JEREMIAH AMBLER & SONS
LIMITED
MOHAIR AND WORSTED SPINNERS
MIDLAND MILLS · BRADFORD.

SPINNERS OF MOHAIR, ALPACA, CAMEL HAIR,
MERINO, CROSSBRED, BRAID, DRESS, COATING,
HOSIERY, CARPET & HAIR CLOTH, YARNS,
COLOURED BOTANY & FANCY YARNS, ETC

MANUFACTURERS OF PRESSCLO
FOR SEED CRUSHING PURPOS
MOHAIR AND ALPACA RUGS

DIRECTORS:
MAJOR E. BEDDINGTON BEHRENS, M.C., PH.D., (CHAIRMAN).
COLONEL LORD BARNBY, C.M.G., C.B.E., M.V.O., (DEPUTY CHAIRMAN).
SIR COLIN McVEAN GUBBINS, K.C.M.G., D.S.O., M.C.
J. S. AMBLER (MANAGING DIRECTOR).

OUR REFCE.

YOUR REFCE.

Saturday June 18th

Dear Pat & John

I know you say you have contacts in
and but just in case I give you the following
MISS. PEGGY. JANE. KOLFF   VAN DE HEIM STRAAT 76 THE HAGUE
I can't now find her phone number & it may be under
mother in the Directory. She is a very good friend of
mine, speaks English like a native. I hope we shall
join up with her in our travels, I've written to her abo
you both.

The other address & who your mother knows

FRANS & MIES (HIS WIFE) DE HAES   MERELLAAN 23 EINDHOVEN
TELEFOON (K4900) 3165   TELEGRAMS TE-TE-BE EINDHOVEN.

well thats that. I've just sent all my papers
for our foreign tour. bar documents etc

In haste & here to all.
Much
Juck

IMPATIENTLY LOOKING FORWARD TO YOU BOTH H

AND LOVE FROM = GRAN AND UNCLE + +

86

OPPOSITE Letter from Uncle Jack received just before we left by train to meet our ship in Quebec. Once we reached England in 1949, he paid all our expenses. Note letterhead of family mill founded in 1789. After Granddad died, Uncle Jack became Managing Director. Not long afterwards, the family no longer owned the mill; the bank did. It was later used as a set for the movie *Room at the Top*.

ABOVE My grandfather Sam Ambler, whom we called Grandad, was a Yorkshire manufacturer, owner of Jeremiah Ambler and Sons, mohair spinners, in Bradford, and a natty fellow who traced his lineage back to a Frenchman who invaded England with William the Conqueror. Full of mischief, he could be frightening at times and once donned a false moustache and nose and chased me round the dining room table. His wife Emily, whom John and I called Gran, was an accomplished pianist of concert ability. Hearing her play was one of the delights of my childhood, as it was also for my mother.

BELOW John and I planned on taking a fishing boat from Holland to England. Uncle Jack was horrified and sent money for a ferry with this welcoming telegram.

OYED CROSSING OUR WELCOME

1469　42/40 NL　BERKELEY CALIF　APRIL 6 1949

RICIA FISHER CARE FISHER SMITH

CAMINO ELMOLINO PO 143 CAPISTRANO BEACH CALIF

VE PASSAGE ON SS TIBITA ROUND TRIP $280.00 LEAVE JULY 7 QUEBEC

RRIVE BACK SEPT 2 NEW YORK. SHORT BUT TIME FOR PENNA AND NEW ENG

ERY INEXPENSIVE. IF OK PLEASE WIRE $150.00 FOR DEPOSITS IMMEDIA

I WILL SELL CAR

JOHN

O P P O S I T E John and I hiking in the Lake District, summer 1949. I was
nineteen and going to Scripps; he was twenty-two, just out of the Army and
studying architecture on the G.I. Bill at U.C. Berkeley.

T O P John booked passage for us on a Dutch student ship, the *Tabita,* which
had been a troop ship. It later sank (and no wonder!), but we had fun.

L E F T Hoyle Court after the war—my room is second from left with windows
wide open. Viney was still there, but now he had no helpers so the flowers from
the herbaceous border had seeded themselves into the lawn and the whole thing
had gone wild.

R I G H T While hiking on the moors above Hoyle Court I picked a sprig of
heather and John snapped my photo. I still have that sprig of heather.

bouquets of fragrant old-fashioned roses mixed with gypsophila. Golden sunshine shone into the room, birds sang in the Virginia creeper. I ached with a mixture of joy in that moment and the pain of yearning for an era that never would return.

When John and I explored the gardens, we found the bird cages empty and standing open. Gretchen the monkey had gone to a real zoo. Our lovely green parrot had died of a cold after Cook had put it in the drafty hall to punish it for swearing. The formal lawn around the lily pond had become a meadow, and the border flowers had seeded themselves into it. Most wonderful was the topiary. No one had pruned it during or since the war. If you looked carefully you could still see the ghost of a ship in one unkempt shrub and the wings of a bird in another. Statues and balustrades overgrown with climbers reminded me of my wisteria far away in California. A year or two later Uncle Jack decided that it was a shame to let Hoyle Court deteriorate, so he sold the house to five masonic temples and the grounds to a condominium project, but the formal gardens were preserved. After a magical summer in England, France, and Holland I returned to Scripps College with renewed energy and ran upstairs to see my new room. But when I threw open the French doors, my eyes fell on a bare balcony.

They had chopped down my wisteria! Every last sinew of that lovely vine had been stripped away, and the ground where it once grew was now paved over. I hunted for the gardeners, though they could hardly conjure a mammoth old vine back to life. The reason for cutting the vine was simple: It had broken the tiles, and the roof was leaking.

Is it any wonder that when Lou and I built our home in Del Mar thirty-eight years ago, the first vine I yearned to plant was a wisteria? But I certainly didn't want to have a problem with our roof, so several years passed before I found the right spot. You can train wisterias as small trees, as shrubs, or even ground covers, but I wanted to grow mine as a climbing vine. It wasn't until John Lloyd Wright and I built a lath structure to give us some shade from the strong west sun that I finally had a place to grow it. When John and I finished our project, it was June. It's always best to purchase wisterias bareroot in January or while they're in bloom in spring, so you can be sure you get the color you want—pink, white, lavender, purple, or blue. In coastal California most wisterias bloom in March, but I was in the mood for planting now. I went to McPherson's Nursery in Encinitas and asked for a purple wisteria.

According to the nurseryman, all the purple wisterias were on one side of a path and the white ones were on the other. I took a purple one on faith, and never even asked if it was the Chinese or the Japanese species. Nor did I ask for a good variety that was grafted or grown from a cutting, instead of from a seed. Like most people who buy plants, I didn't know what I was doing; I just plunged in. Most people, for example, don't know that Chinese wisterias *(Wisteria sinensis)* bloom all at once, giving a spectacular show on bare wood before the leaves emerge. By contrast, the blossoms of Japanese wisterias *(W. floribunda)* open at the same time that the leaves are emerging and then the individual flowers open slowly from top to bottom.

Although the bloom display of Japanese wisterias is less overwhelmingly colorful than that of Chinese wisterias, it usually lasts longer. Some Japanese wisterias have extraordinarily long racemes—much longer than Chinese ones—and it's possible to get named varieties with superior characteristics. It's unfortunate that gardeners often plant a wisteria, a plant that's going to live for many years—perhaps for centuries—without realizing that all the best ones are grafted or grown from cuttings. Seed-grown plants are inferior in color and may not bloom for several years after planting. There are other types of wisteria available but less frequently found in nurseries, including the lovely, large-flowered, and very fragrant silky wisteria *(W. venusta)*.

I took my mystery wisteria home and prepared to plant it outside my daughter Wendy's bedroom window on the corner of the lath structure. The soil in that spot was far from ideal. It consisted of eight inches of top soil covering a subsoil of red clay that was more like stone than soil. Water will drain through this rocklike subsoil eventually but at a depressingly slow rate. To make matters worse the spot was at that time on the edge of a lawn requiring frequent irrigation. Wisterias will grow in just about any soil, but they need good drainage. That much I knew.

In those days, many garden books advised the digging of sumps, so like many other well-intentioned but poorly informed gardeners faced with a drainage problem, I built a sump. I dug a huge planting hole, removing two and a half feet of red sandstone, and hauling it away. Then using a crowbar and a posthole digger, I dug a narrower and deeper hole in the center of it. I filled this narrow hole with crushed rock. This was the sump. (I was still in my twenties, so my ignorance of the right way to provide drainage was combined with abundant energy and brute strength.) I covered the bottom of the planting hole with a layer of top soil mixed with organic soil amendment, placed the rootball of my cherished wisteria into the hole, and backfilled the hole with more of the topsoil mixture. You can just imagine how virtuous I felt when I'd finished this exhausting work.

It never occurred to me that all the drainage water from rain or irrigation would quite naturally percolate down through the lovely top soil mixture, collect in the sump, and then just sit there like a hidden swimming pool, waiting for my wisteria's roots to plunge in and rot. Fortunately, sumps have now been widely discredited. Most people realize they only collect water; they don't drain it away.

Chimney drains are different. They're made just like sumps with one enormous difference: the small hole in the bottom of the planting hole goes all the way through the hardpan or buried rock layer into a layer of soil that drains, which was impossible in my garden because the red clay layer is many feet thick. It would have been better to plant straight into the native soil than to do what I did. The best solution in similar cases is to build a raised bed. Digging gypsum into the red clay on the bottom of the planting hole is another way to help increase the drainage in clay soil when its failure to drain is caused by alkalinity. Gypsum helps break up alkaline soils and make them drain better; it won't do any harm and may help.

Despite the mistakes I made when I planted my first wisteria, it seemed happy at first and grasped life with eager tendrils. It grew so rapidly that I was kept busy that first summer training it on wires in the gap between the house and the lath. For the first two years it didn't bloom, and I was quite disgusted. Then when the wisteria was three years old, it finally covered itself with fat flower buds. At last! I thought, but when they opened, what a disappointment. The flowers weren't purple; they were white. I told myself that white flowers are always lovely and more sophisticated than brilliantly colorful ones. Vita Sackville-West had said so; who was I to disagree? But my heart was set on purple like the vine they'd cut down at Scripps. My white wisteria was a Japanese variety with long narrow racemes, and its flowers were unusually fragile. Shortly after they opened, we had a heavy wind and rain and most of them shattered.

By the following year the enterprising vine had grown from one end of the patio to the other. That spring we had some warm weather, and the fringe-like flowers came out all at once in a massive display under a lacy covering of light green leaves. When the blossoms were at the height of bloom, a friend happened to drop by. She stepped through the gate into the patio and gasped.

"Oh, Pat, I've never seen a more beautiful wisteria!"

"Yes," I agreed, "It is beautiful, but it's white. I wish it were purple."

CHINESE WISTERIAS, COVERED with purple blooms in March, festoon the pergola that shades the brick walk leading to our front door.

Almost right away the blossoms began to wilt, and the very next day they fell off. No sooner had the blossoms fallen than the leaves began to turn yellow. Within a week they had fallen too. The vine shriveled and died to the ground. Bad drainage or not, I knew I'd killed it with a cruel word.

I didn't have the heart to try growing another wisteria, so I sawed off the trunk at ground level and planted annual flowers next to where it had grown. About six years later Raymundo, my trusty helper, started working for me one day a week, as he still does today. I asked him to dig up the woody stump of the old wisteria and all the dead roots that had been too difficult for me to remove. He did his usual thorough job, and several years went by. Then one day a friend asked me if I ever talked to my plants.

"I don't think I actually talk aloud to them, but I do communicate with them mentally. Sometimes I hug trees. Also," I added ruefully, "I once killed a white wisteria with a cruel word. It grew right over here outside Wendy's window. I still feel very sorry that I criticized it."

Well, would you believe that a day or two later a tiny green sprout popped up? It took off like a rocket, grew straight up and wound around a beam. The next spring Wendy, now in her teens, came dashing into the kitchen. "Mother!" she cried, "A miracle! The wisteria is blooming and it's PURPLE!"

That wisteria is still alive today. Some people to whom I tell this story don't believe it, but there is an explanation. All white varieties of wisteria are grafted onto purple rootstocks, which are more vigorous. So, it is my belief that although the white—or grafted—portions of my plant died along with most of the roots, a tiny piece of the orginal purple rootstock must have survived. When I said I was sorry, perhaps I gave it the energy to grow.

If you decide to plant your own wisteria, there are a few additional things you should know. During the first few years after planting, you should water and feed it adequately. After three years, you can water less and stop feeding. Mature wisterias that aren't watered too much usually bloom better. Also, young wisterias send out a great many long twining shoots. Train and tie these onto your support to make the framework of your vine. If you want the vine to grow up posts, start all the twiners in one direction, so you don't get a muddled looking web of crisscrossing growth.

Once your basic structure is arranged, you can begin cutting off all unwanted streamers back to two buds or leaf nodes. This will make the plant grow more spur wood, which will give you more flowers the following spring. Spurs are short, stubby, somewhat twisted pieces of wood that jut out from the smoother structural wood of the vine. (Apple trees flower from spurs and so do wisterias.) Don't cut off the spurs or you'll destroy all your bloom. You can also distinguish the spurs from the twiners in winter by the fat flower buds they carry. Leaf buds are narrower. Smooth, long twining wood bears lots of leaf buds but few or no flower buds. Each time you prune off some streamers in summer back to one or two buds, you'll also get an immediate bonus; the vine will reward you by sporting a few summer blooms.

Following these guidelines, I've planted and grown many wisterias in our garden, including a row of purple Chinese ones on our entryway pergola, each of which is a fine grafted specimen. So, you see, at last I have that glorious wisteria I yearned for back in my college days.

8.

A Valley Filled with Daffodils

MOST LARGE-TRUMPET daffodils do not multiply readily in the coastal zones of Southern California. Nonetheless, I often plant them to remind myself of how in spring their happy blossoms fill the Valley of the Wharfe at Bolton Abbey in Yorkshire. Bolton Abbey, as we used to call it—or Bolton Priory as it's correctly called today—isn't as well-known as the more spectacular Fountains Abbey, but it's hard to imagine a more charming spot. When Lou and I visited the place with our children in the summer of 1969, the daffodil season was over, but pink hawthorns bloomed next to a tumbled wall. Cows meandered through the ruins, munching grass inside the roofless chancel.

We had stopped for lunch at the Devonshire Arms, a hotel famous for its good lunches and hearty teas. "To reach the abbey," the pleasant man at the front desk told us, "look for a hole in the wall across the road and a little further up. Enter there and follow the footpath."

We scrambled down the muddy path, hanging onto the pipe railing and sliding down the last stretch—the worst bit, which unaccountably had no railing—without landing in the mud. Then the slope became gentler, and we passed the hunting lodge of the Duke of Devonshire on the edge of the woods. In the distance we saw the ruins of Bolton Priory, pillaged and burned by order of Henry VIII. Below the soaring ruins flowed the wide and lovely River Wharfe, sparkling clear. You could cross it by a footbridge or by enormous stepping stones. I wanted to leap across them but they were too far apart.

When I was a child, this was a favorite picnic spot, especially in spring when daffodils nodded their yellow heads in great drifts around the abbey. After lunch, we used to hike upstream to a place called "the Strid" where bluebells carpet the woods in spring and the river roars through a narrow chasm far below. Foolhardy people—it's said the son of the founder of Bolton Priory was among them—have attempted to leap across the narrow gap and have fallen to their deaths. My cousin Monica, who has always been interested in history, told John and me that the bluebells were native but the daffodils were introduced in the Middle Ages. "A Cistercian friar brought a handful of bulbs from France," she said, "and planted them under a tree. The winters were mild in those times, so the bulbs multiplied and slowly crept across the whole valley. During mild years they slept safely through the winter beneath a blanket of snow and survived to bloom again in spring. But when arctic air swept down

WHEN FRANCIE, WENDY, Lou and I visited this spot in the summer of 1969, the hawthorns were covered with pink blossoms. Further up the river there are usable stepping stones; those here have been augmented by a footbridge.

from the north as it did in the fourteenth century and stayed long enough to freeze the ground, all the bulbs in the open were killed. Only the bulbs that were protected beneath the trees where the friars had first planted them survived. Then slowly over the years, they crept out again until once more they crossed the valley. That's what's been happening here, over and over again, for hundreds of years."

When I was young I used to wonder what the difference was between a daffodil and a narcissus. They seemed to be the same thing. Eventually, I learned that indeed they were, but that daffodil is the common name for narcissus, while narcissus is the botanical name for a huge tribe of spring-blooming bulbs native to Europe and North Africa. Although all narcissuses can correctly be lumped together under the common name daffodil, the Tazetta and Tazetta hybrid narcissus—including paper whites, Chinese sacred lilies, Grand Soleil d'Or, and others—are never separately called by the common name. For some illogical reason, gardeners and bulb catalogs alike usually call these narcissuses (or narcissi if you prefer the Latin plural).

The flowers of Tazetta narcissuses are highly fragrant, and they're polyanthus, that is, they bear many tiny flowers in bunches on each stem. In mild climates such as Southern California, we put them in the ground in September or October and in a few weeks they bloom. Inland, where it's a bit colder, they wait until spring. Paperwhites start to bloom as early as November in my garden, and a large clump of golden Grand Soleil d'Or blooms for several months from fall to spring.

The main way the Tazetta group differs from all other narcissuses is that they aren't hardy. They can survive the light frosts we have in Southern California, but they can't survive a long cold winter. All the other narcissuses—the ones we commonly call daffodils—are hardy; they can usually survive in cold-winter climates as long as the ground itself doesn't freeze. Fortunately, however, gardeners in all parts of the country can enjoy Tazetta narcissuses indoors in winter by forcing them into bloom in water and pebbles. Good candidates are paper whites, Chinese sacred lilies, Cragford, and Grand Soleil d'Or. By planting them six weeks before you want the flowers, as I have often done, you can have them in bloom for Thanksgiving or Christmas.

In spring when yellow daffodils bloom in our garden, Lou sometimes reminds me that in Chicago they were called jonquils. They may well have been jonquils, but in my garden they usually aren't. Jonquil is the botanical name for just one division of daffodils—*Narcissus jonquilla*. Jonquils are prized for their strong fragrance. They bloom late and are usually yellow with short cups on a foot-high stem. Their leaves are round like reeds instead of straplike like most other narcissuses. Trevithian is the best known variety, but one very hardy species from the Atlas Mountains, *Narcissus watieri,* bears large white flowers on six-inch stems and doesn't seem to mind moderately dry summers. The early settlers brought jonquils to Chicago where they thrived. Thus in many parts of the Midwest, all narcissuses came to be known incorrectly as jonquils.

After my family emigrated to the United States, my mother bought a farm in Bucks County, Pennsylvania. Windyridge Farm stood on the side of a gentle hill and was not particularly windy. One of the first things she and Geoff did was to plant six or eight bulbs under each of the trees that stood in the lawn. Five years later, when we left the farm, that small handful of bulbs under each tree had multiplied so abundantly that each tree was surrounded by a thick yellow mat of flowers in spring. After the blooms faded, we clipped off the faded flowers, leaving the stems to send their juices down into the bulb. When the long, straplike leaves drooped, we gathered them into bunches and tied a knot in them so they wouldn't look untidy. We allowed the grass to grow long around these knotted leaves until the daffodil leaves had gone completely brown. Then we pulled them off and mowed close to the tree again. Daffodils need their green leaves to gain strength for the following year.

Even though daffodils are hardy bulbs, they don't require a freezing winter in order to bloom, so they're easy to grow in mild climates. Unlike hyacinths, crocuses, and tulips, they don't need six weeks of chilling in the

SPRINGTIME ON OUR patio—King Alfred daffodils with hyacinths and Iceland poppies.

refrigerator prior to planting. But one cannot expect daffodils to last for centuries in California the way they do in England or in the eastern portions of the United States. (In Virginia daffodils planted in colonial times still bloom every spring.) Nonetheless, a few varieties naturalize quite readily in Southern California and eventually make big clumps—February Gold is one of these. For the most part, I buy daffodils as a one-time splurge, counting the flowers I get in subsequent years as an added bonus. I buy daffodils almost every year because to me no other flowers are so expressive of spring.

I purchase my bulbs in the fall, store them in a cool dry place such as the garage, and plant them in November or in December, when the weather's cooler. I always buy No. 1 grade bulbs, choosing the best and biggest ones in the bin. I feel each one carefully to make sure it's solid and heavy. Soft bulbs are partially rotted, and light ones are dried out. It's worth paying extra for double- or triple-nose bulbs. In warm-winter climates we don't pull our bulbs apart; we plant them as one bulb and each nose or point gives us a bloom.

Choose a spot with good drainage in full sun or part shade. The flowers will turn toward the sun, so don't plant them where their backs will face you. Dig the soil deeply, mix in soil amendment, and rake the ground level. Then with a trowel make individual holes a little more than twice as deep as the height of the bulb. Put a tablespoon of bone meal in the bottom of each hole, cover this with some soil, and place the bulb with the roots facing down and the point facing up in the bottom of the hole. Fill the hole with soil and press it down gently with your hand. After planting, the bottom of bulb should be twice as deep as the height of the bulb. If you prefer, you can skip the bone meal and feed your bulbs instead with a balanced fertilizer especially formulated for bulbs. It's more fuss to use, but it contains nitrogen to feed the bulb and will give good results if used according to package directions.

If you have many bulbs to plant, you can dig out a section of prepared earth in the shape of a graceful drift. Outline the drift with gypsum, and then dig out the soil to the recommended depth. If you choose to feed your bulbs with bone meal, sprinkle some in the bottom of your planting hole and then cover this with a layer of soil before placing the bulbs in the trench or tossing them into it. Avoid planting daffodils in rows. For a natural look, toss them on the ground and plant them where they fall.

In my garden, I cannot reproduce the great drifts of daffodils one sees in colder climates. Nor do I want to. We Californians can carpet the ground with orange poppies and sky-blue lupines. But let me always have at least one yellow daffodil in spring. One happy yellow face to waft me back to Wharfedale, where pebbles glint beneath clear water, where stepping stones stand too far apart for crossing, and cows graze among the ruins.

TROUBLESHOOTING

A VIEW OF the *tsukubai* and one of the cranes in the Japanese garden the Teagues helped me build outside Lou's and my bedroom window.

9.

The Japanese Garden
That Was Built in One Day

ONE CAN TELL oneself that a certain amount of mess is a natural part of gardening—it's unrealistic to expect every room in a garden to look like a magazine photograph every day of the year—but there does come a time when one has to stop stalling and revamp an area that's gone sour. A few years ago, a large flower bed edging the patio outside our bedroom window became completely clogged with sword ferns. I'd planted those ferns thirty years previously from a handful of leaves and roots given to me by my dear friend Jane Roe. Jane and her husband Richard have five children, one of whom is Hilary Metternich, whose house we rent in France. Jane is also an avid gardener. "Sword ferns can be invasive," she warned. "Keep an eye on them or they'll take over."

For many years, my sword ferns didn't live up to their reputation; they just sat there doing nothing. Then, without warning, they burst into action and crowded out all the other plants in the bed. They eventually grew to be tall, lush, and tropical looking. For some years, I put up with them, until finally the bed was so full of sword ferns that they began to strangle each other and turned from glorious green to yucky yellow. At last I couldn't stand those ferns any longer, so I asked Raymundo to dig them all out and refill the area with fresh top soil from the compost pile.

Meanwhile, I dreamed of replacing the ferns with a small Japanese garden, but how would I ever accomplish it? Part of my inspiration lay hidden away in a closet in the form of three bronze Japanese cranes that Lou had inherited. Two of them were badly bent and wouldn't stand up, but I thought they could be mended. Elsewhere in the garden was another inspiration, a stone lotus-shaped water basin, a genuine *tsukubai* from Japan; I'd bought it years ago from a kind neighbor who was moving away and wanted me to have it. I tried to visualize a small teahouse garden incorporating these objects, but it takes special talent and know-how to make a Japanese garden that doesn't look artificial or contrived. I wished I could find someone with that gift.

It was then that fate took a hand; a friend introduced me to Bill and Linda Teague, whose Del Mar garden is based on, but not imitative of, a Japanese garden. I told them my plan and showed them the space. I'd sculpted the soil into a hill at one end and shaped a dry pond next to it that I intended to fill with blue beach rocks gathered many years ago. The Teagues were enthusiastic and with generosity offered to help.

"The first step is to assemble all the plants and rocks and art objects we'll need," Bill explained. "Place them right here on the patio where they'll be close at hand. Take your beach rocks and sort them in three piles—small, middle-sized, and large—then line up the plants. Perhaps you could find some variegated liriope, some big blue liriope, and some of the smaller kinds of heavenly bamboo—Nandina 'Nana' or 'Compacta' and 'Filimentosa.' I'll bring black mondo grass, dwarf mondo grass, various ferns, and three heights of bamboo. You'd better get a drain tile to contain the ground-cover variety of bamboo; it's very invasive. The others won't be a problem."

"How about these plants I already have?" I showed him a rhapis palm, an aspidistra, a bonsai sago palm, and a large-scale bonsai deodar cedar. "Anything like that will be great," he replied.

I needed a piece of hollow bamboo to carry water into the fountain, so I asked the Teagues if I could get a length of bamboo from their garden and hollow it out myself. "We tried that once," said Linda, "but it wasn't easy. You're welcome to use our bamboo if you want, but it would be much simpler to buy a ready-made *shishi-odoshi,* or deer scare. We'll just use the portion that drips water into the container." Linda told me I should be able to find one in San Francisco or at a Japanese hardware store in Los Angeles. "And while you're there," she added, "you can pick up a section of ornamental bamboo fence and a *shishaku,* a bamboo water scoop."

"When you've gathered all the ingredients," said Bill, "phone us and we'll come over and finish the garden in one day." Then he said something that made a deep impression on me. "You see, making a Japanese garden is rather like baking a cake. First, you gather the ingredients— that's the time consuming part—and then you put it all together and that part goes quite quickly."

The next week, I happened to go to Los Angeles on business. While I was there, I detoured to a Japanese hardware store and bought the water scoop, the *shishi-odoshi,* and the bamboo fence, their very last section. I took the cranes to a blacksmith to be mended. Raymundo moved the water basin and some large lichen-covered rocks from other places where they'd never be missed. I gathered blue rocks from elsewhere in the garden and sorted them by size into three piles. Finally, I purchased the plants. When all the ingredients were assembled, I phoned the Teagues to invite them over.

PHOTO OF THE patio and table where we had lunch that day.

On the following Sunday, a beautiful August day, Bill and Linda arrived laden with plants. No sooner had we lined them up with the other ingredients than Bill dropped into a silent trance that apparently endowed his tall slim frame with the strength of a Japanese wrestler. Slowly and deliberately, he hefted the rocks, some of them weighing more than he did, and rooted each one in the perfect spot, so that it looked as if it had always been there. Meanwhile, I buried a drip line, connected it to a water source, and threaded it through the *shishi-odoshi*, while Linda separated clumps of dwarf mondo grass blade by blade and laboriously planted each tiny rooted specimen an inch apart. "If you do it this way," she explained, "it spreads into a beautiful carpet with the leaves facing this way and that."

At noon Lou joined us for lunch around the patio table. By day's end, the garden was finished. Plants, rocks, cranes were all in place. Water dripped restfully from the *shishi-odoshi* into the water basin. Blue beach rocks in three sizes were arranged to indicate expanding circles in a peaceful pond. Then Linda produced a little bundle of black bamboo she'd brought from home; four pieces of various lengths and thicknesses were knotted together at each end with black twine. She laid the bundle on the edge of the water basin and rested the bamboo scoop across it.

"Now this is what you do when you come home," she said. "You step on this rock, pick up the scoop, and fill it with a little water. The *tsukubai* is placed low on purpose so you have to bend down to express your humility. The Japanese would probably sip a little water from the scoop, but you can if you wish just pour some of it into the palm of one hand. Replace the scoop, and then wash both your hands in the water from your palm. Shake off the rest of the droplets onto the plants and brush a little moisture lightly over your hair. Now you're ready to go into the house leaving all the troubles of the world behind you."

Including any problems in the garden, I thought. I drank in the serenity of the rocks, the plants, the dripping water. What had begun as a dream had become a reality, just as Bill had said it would. At last I understood what he'd meant when he said "making a Japanese garden is rather like baking a cake." Once we'd assembled the ingredients, we'd put them all together in a single day.

10.

A Troublesome Spot
Where Nothing Would Grow

SHORTLY AFTER LOU and I built our home in Del Mar, I chose what I thought was the perfect place for planting a bed of annual flowers. A level area next to the drive, it was about six feet wide, ten feet long, and in full sun. The far end was framed by a knoll of red rock and a native toyon tree. There was room for a path at the back, and the steep bank beyond it was held up by a mammoth log, all that was left of a felled eucalyptus. Someone had sawed off the smaller limbs and left the lower sections, including several large scaffold branches, lying sideways on the ground. Then the rains came and filled in the earth behind it. I peeled off the rotting bark to reveal the hard smooth wood, and— presto—it became a striking garden accent.

The ground I chose for the flowerbed was loose and sandy. I spaded it with ease to the depth of a foot or so and then mixed in a bag of soil amendment and an appropriate amount of granulated fertilizer recommended for flowerbeds. Then I watered the bed and and let it settle while I went to the nursery. It was fall so I bought a selection of cool-season flowers—pansies, snapdragons, Johnny-jump-ups, Iceland poppies, stock, calendulas, primroses, and sweet alyssum. Here in coastal zones of California we can plant cool-season flowers in September through November. They bloom all winter right through spring until they're cut down by hot weather.

Down on my knees planting my first flowerbed in our new garden, I was in a sort of heaven, my head filled with a vision of the finished product. When the gardener's heart is filled with hope, all the work seems fun and easy. Once the bed was planted, I sent it good thoughts, watered it regularly, and waited for it to bloom. Imagine my dismay, then, when all the plants—even the sweet alyssum—turned yellow, shriveled up, and died. It looked like a case of root rot, but why would the flowers have died from root rot when the drainage appeared to be good? Taking one pathetic dead little plant as an example, I went back to the nursery, related my tragic tale to the owner, and asked what I'd done wrong.

"You overwatered," he said. But he took pity on me and pressed a flat of gazanias into my hands. "Try these. I guarantee you won't be able to kill gazanias, but let the ground dry out a little between waterings." Then as an afterthought he reached for a bottle of Terrovite. "I'd buy this if I were you and feed your gazanias with it to get them started. It's kind of a miracle fertilizer for everything that grows in California except California native plants. They don't like it."

I planted those gazanias right away, cared for them lovingly, checked the soil with a trowel to make sure I neither over- or under-watered them, and fed them Terrovite. The nurseryman was right; it's often a miracle fertilizer for troubled western soils. But even Terrovite didn't save my gazanias; they too keeled over and died. I was too embarrassed to complain a second time, so on my own I tried a flat of ivy, the toughest of all tough plants, I reasoned, but it too gave up the ghost.

It never occurred to me to have a soil test. Looking back, it might or might not have helped. If my problem had been caused by extreme alkalinity, acidity, or salinity, a soil test could have solved the mystery. But it's possible, too, that there was a large percentage of unrotted organic matter in the ground—perhaps raw sawdust from the eucalyptus tree—and so even though I fertilized more than once I may have failed to add adequate nitrogen. If soil contains a high percentage of unrotted carbonaceous organic matter, this will rob nitrogen from the soil thus killing plants. To prevent this from happening, you need to add extra nitrogen. For example, if you were to spread a layer of raw sawdust one-inch deep over 100 square feet of earth, you would need to sprinkle one pound of ammonium sulfate all over it before tilling it into the ground. Also, some plants are allelopathic, or death-dealing; they tend to poison the ground around them to cut down on competition. Eucalyptus is one of these and acacia is another. A soil test wouldn't uncover this effect.

I didn't have time or patience just then for unravelling mysteries. I simply decided that for some unknown reason that spot was barren, covered it with blue beach rocks to make it look like a dry pond in a Japanese garden, and chose another spot for planting flowers. Years went by and then one day a truck rattled up the drive and several workmen piled out.

"An old water main goes through your property right here under these beach rocks," the foreman said. "Good thing you haven't planted anything here because every once in a while, like now, we need to dig down and inspect the pipe."

An iron pipe twelve or eighteen inches thick and somewhat rusty with black paint peeling off it lay just below that mysterious spot where nothing would grow. If I'd looked on our plot plan I'd have seen the easement. If I'd dug a little deeper I'd have struck it with my spade. You wouldn't think that a pipe would prevent plants above it from growing, but perhaps it did. I've heard of occasions when a large buried boulder has had the same effect. And it isn't only rocks. Sometimes cement, paint thinner, or plaster have been dumped onto the ground and covered up.

Roots from invasive plants—trees and groundcovers, particularly— can also create soil that's so hard and dry it's impossible to add a new plant and expect it to grow. I've coped with this problem so many times that I finally came up with a solution I call "the pot trick." You can use it with plants as small as annual flowers or as large as shrubs and trees— anything that will survive in a container.

My mother and Bill Begley once gave me several camellias and aza- leas that had grown too big for the small garden surrounding their retirement home. At that time the only area I had for growing them was under some pine trees where the ground was covered with Algerian ivy—far too invasive a companion for camellias and azaleas. So with the help of Raymundo, I planted the shrubs in acid soil mix in some ugly plastic containers we happened to have on hand. Then we cut away cir- cles of ivy, dug holes in the ground slightly larger than the tubs, and placed a large stepping stone on the bottom of each. Finally, we sank the tubs into the holes. When we'd finished, the effect was just as if the plants were growing in the ground. We kept those camellias and azaleas growing in their tubs for ten years until eventually we pulled out all the ivy and transplanted them into the ground where they grow today, mulched with pine needles and watered by a drip system.

To keep a camellia growing indefinitely in a tub, put it on its side and slip it out of its container in late spring, just after it finishes bloom- ing and before it begins to grow. With a sharp knife, slice two inches off the roots from two opposite sides of the root ball. Then slip the root ball back into the tub and refill the empty two inches on each side with fresh acid soil mix, tamping it down well with a stick. Finish by lightly cutting back the foliage—an inch or two off the longest branches is ample. The following year take the plant out of the tub again and slice off the roots on the two sides of the root ball you previously left uncut, and continue year after year, always alternating sides.

My favorite use of the pot trick is to create the look of a flower bed in ground where invasive roots from trees or other plants would make it impossible to grow flowers. Such places abound in old gardens in many parts of the United States and Europe. Here's how to solve the problem: First, choose bushy flowers that are adapted to semi-shade—impatiens and begonias are ideal. You will need to purchase them already growing in six- or eight-inch plastic containers or, alternatively, pot up an adequate number of flowers in containers of this size.

The next step is to dig holes to receive them. First, turn an empty container of the same size you have chosen upside down on the surface of the ground. Cut around it down into the ground with a keyhole saw or old kitchen knife, then remove the pot, dig out the earth from the precut hole with a trowel and put it in a bucket to discard later in some other spot in the garden. When you are working under trees such as cypress and eucalyptus that have many small surface roots, you will find the task involves pulling out a mat of these roots by hand rather than digging out earth. In the case of some trees, such as blue spruce or cedar, there may be many large roots lying exposed on top of the soil. Don't cut into these large roots; instead, dig your holes between them. Make each hole three or four inches deeper than the pot it is to hold, and then slip in one of your pre-planted containers.

Continue digging holes and placing pots in a diamond pattern at appropriate intervals of six inches to one foot depending on the eventual size of your plants. Finally, cover the bare ground between the pots with mulch. The plants will soon fill in and cover the mulched area just as if they were growing in the ground. From time to time remove the

IMPATIENS SURROUNDING MY garden gnome. I planted them in pots sunk into the ground and watered with a drip system.

pots and pull out tree roots that will doubtless try to sneak in from the bottom. Add a drip system if you wish.

The pot trick is not suitable for use under such trees as avocado, citrus, or California live oaks that are subject to crown rot, trunk rot, or root rot. But under eucalyptus, cypress, melaleuca, acacia, pine, spruce, cedar, and many other trees, it works like a dream. Once when Lou and I were in Florence, we visited the gardens of the Medici villas. Next to the main pathway in one of those gardens, under the spreading branches of a venerable cedar tree, the grass had worn away and the soil had become hard, dry, and unsightly. But the gardeners had planted close to a hundred small agaves, aloes, and other succulents in six-inch clay pots and then sunk these pots up to their rims between the surface roots under the tree. The result was a carpet of green growth that didn't endanger the roots of the tree and seldom needed water.

VEGETABLE GARDENING

11.

The Last Two Century Plants
in the Whole World

I

T'S GREAT FUN to grow one's own vegetables, but it's more than fun. It's the very soul of gardening, where it all began. I learned this early in life—not from books on garden history, but from experience. It was woven into the very warp and woof of a lifestyle in which gardens, gardening, and communion with nature played a stellar part.

First, there was Grandad's vegetable garden at Hoyle Court. Never before or since have I tasted tomatoes so indescribably delicious as those that Viney grew in Grandad's greenhouses—it was too cold in Yorkshire for growing them outdoors. Grandad often plucked a bright red, warm, shiny fruit straight from the vine and handed it to me. When I put my nose flat on it to breathe in its pungent aroma he'd nudge me. "Don't inhale it, loov, eat it!" And its juice ran down my face.

Viney and his staff did all the work, but Grandad took notice of everything that went on in the garden just as he did in the kitchen. It was Grandad, not Gran, who consulted with Cook in the morning and

ABOVE Tea al fresco at Chess Cottage with Mum and Bill and some of the silver Mum later sold in her antique shop on the Sunset Strip in Hollywood, which she opened to help support the family.
RIGHT The author with Tinker, our Sealyham terrier, in front of Geoff's abundantly productive vegetable garden at Chess Cottage.

chose the dinner menu, ranging from grouse in season, curried lamb, or roast beef and Yorkshire pudding to bakewell or treacle tarts or Cook's scrumptious Toffee Pudding served with cream. Last of all came a wheel of the finest Stilton cheese and, for the grownups, walnuts and a glass of port.

And the vegetables! At Hoyle Court we devoured glistening mounds of the tiniest of peas, the crunchiest of beans. We consumed the sweetest young carrots ever rolled in butter and sprinkled with chopped parsley, the tastiest new potatoes done the same way, the tenderest and most fragrant vegetable marrows ever stuffed. Our vegetables were picked the day they were consumed and never overcooked. Only Gran failed to join into the general enthusiasm for food around the Ambler dinner table. From her end of the table facing Grandad but miles away from him, she watched the rest of us with controlled distaste, pushing a small piece of Dover sole around with her fork and following it up with an herbal drink called Slippery Elm.

The vegetable garden at Hoyle Court and the dining-room table where we ate its produce were only a beginning. Later, there was our immediate family's first vegetable garden behind the kitchen at Chess Cottage. There was the garden Geoff only dreamed of planting in Huntington, Long Island; the history of potato farming on Pond Island; the kitchen garden already planted and growing in Nyack, New York, when Dad, John, and I moved in. Above all, there was that magnificent vegetable garden at Windyridge Farm with its rows and rows of raspberries and sweet corn and tomatoes and peas and beans and potatoes. That's where my family's passion for growing its own food brought forth an abundant harvest. And finally came California, with a whole new way of growing crops in tune with the seasons. But I'm getting ahead of my story again. I must go back and fill you in.

My mother Ruth divorced Dad and married Geoffrey Morris in 1934. After a year or two at Chess Cottage, she'd almost forgotten she had ever agreed to emigrate with him to America. In April 1936, Mum gave birth to their son Bill. Then one evening in August 1937, out of the clear blue sky, Geoff tossed on the dinner table in front of Mum two one-way tickets on the *Queen Mary* to New York and declared, "We sail in one month!"

"What?" Mum cried in fury. "How could you spring this on me! I can't suddenly drop everything, sell Chess Cottage, make arrangements for the children, and leave for good in one month. For God's sake, Geoff, use

JOHN WITH DAD at the Gleddings. The shelf under the upstairs windows is the one that John and I climbed around to reach Grandma's room when we were very young. The upper window to the right is the very one through which Grandma's maid, Lizzie, safely pulled us.

your head!" Geoff scowled. "All right then. I'll go and you can follow as soon as you can." And there was nothing Mum could do about it.

"War will soon break out between England and Germany," she explained to John and me. "Geoff's work won't do well in wartime, so we're going to emigrate to America, the Land of Opportunity. Geoff and I are going first to make a foothold, and meanwhile you two and Bill will have to stay in England. I expect you both to be very brave—stiff upper lip, remember! It won't be long before we'll be able to send for you." As it turned out it was fifteen months.

Mum sailed to America on the H.M.S. *Georgic* in October 1937. Standing on deck watching England disappear on the horizon, knowing she was leaving three young children behind her, was the worst moment of her life, but she steeled herself and turned her face toward the west. That evening, she experienced a stroke of luck. At a cocktail party she was introduced to Mr. and Mrs. James V. Spadea of New York who were returning from France where they'd been attending the Paris designer shows. They knew Geoff, having met him years earlier in France when he was married to the Paris couturiere, Peggy Morris. Jean Spadea was an Irish beauty and a remarkable artist; her husband Jim, a good-hearted, ebullient Italian with business acumen. The Spadeas owned a fashion sydicate and published a magazine. Jean designed all Lord and Taylor's ads—she'd created the famous rose insignia on the Fifth Avenue awnings. By the end of the voyage, Jean, Jim, and Mum had begun a friendship between our families that has lasted all our lives, and Jim had promised to give Geoff enough work to keep him and Mum afloat.

Meanwhile, Chess Cottage sold quickly, John continued on at Beaumont House, and I lived with Norah and Bill in a flat painted ghastly green inside, but luckily still in Loudwater. I walked to school on the same road past fields where the river meandered peacefully and cows lounged among the buttercups chewing their cuds. I rode the

New Years Eve xxooxxoo Lots of love & kisses and a very
Happy New Year to you all Pat Lois Frankie Wendy Fran
and John. We are having a wonderful time in this fairytale
Blue sky white snow dark Trees a wonderful white Mountain
the lake is all frozen over so we can walk on it. We take the
up and Walk down & if we get tired we can
Take a Sleigh ride like this
we so much enjoyed

watching the international skating and
jumping and
CRESTA 350 M.P.H.
TOBOGGAN RUN
round impossible ice
walls the English Boys seem
to be the most expert at this
and Bob running internal
with 4 people
here
we've also been doing some of this   a gala dance
at the Kulm Hotel with   Josephine
Baker the French Coloured   night club entertainer
and of course we've been up the mountains to
watch them skiing in this kind of a thing

We are now going down to
the Bar to drink your health
the wine here is wonderful &
Cheap we can get it out
of the barrel and the food is wonderful
the Hotel is run by a   family 2 boys a girl
and Moma & Papa   Lots of love from us both
to you all Dad

OPPOSITE Dad was a world traveler. Throughout his life he kept in touch with us by writing amusing letters illustrated with charming little drawings.

ABOVE Dad, Pat, John, and Grandma in the Conservatory, Christmas 1937, with dolls that the ladies of one of Grandma's auxiliaries had dressed in handmade clothes for sale at a charity bazaar.

RIGHT On my ninth birthday, Dad sent me this telegram from Toronto, Canada. Mum and Geoff were in New York at the time.

pony Blackie twice a week and now, as before, we all went back to Yorkshire for the holidays. John and I divided our time between Hoyle Court and the Gleddings. That year we had Christmas with Grandma at the Gleddings, and Dad came home for the holidays all the way from Hollywood where he was working in the movies.

All during 1938 the fear of war heated up. Two German schoolmates of John's at Beaumont House were sent back home; Norah and I took part in air raid drills; I carried a gas mask to school. But when the summer holidays rolled around again, we forgot all that. We spent July at Hoyle Court, and then Grandma sent Alsop, the chauffeur, over with the Rolls to pick us up and take us to Halifax. We'd been looking forward to August at the Gleddings; it was always such a lark. Norah never went with us. Grandma's staff, including Alsop, an Irish maid called Lizzie, and Phoebe the cook, were always joking with us and seemed to enjoy having us around. They left us to our own devices, and sometimes we got into scrapes dreamed up by John, usually with my wholehearted cooperation.

When we were quite young one of John's great ideas—"brain waves" we called them then—was to climb out my bedroom window and surprise Grandma by walking around the corner to her room on a ledge that went all the way around the house under the upstairs windows. It was four or five inches wide and sloped slightly downwards. I said "Take me too or I'll tell."

Hand-in-hand, facing the building, we inched our way around the corner, sliding our feet sideways until we reached Grandma's window. At the dressing table just inside the window Lizzie was brushing Grandma's hair. John knocked on the window, Lizzie peered around the corner and her mouth fell open. Quick as a flash she pulled up the sash and lifted us into the room. Poor Grandma was white as a sheet.

Grandma often took us on outings into the countryside for picnics or to visit historic places; sometimes we stayed in hotels en route. In mid-summer we often drove to wild places high up on the moors where all you could see for miles in every direction were hills stained purple with heather in full bloom. Grandma, all covered with lap rugs and watched over by Alsop, sat in the back of the car like a tender tropical in a glass hothouse, while John and I and our cousins Harriet and Monica, who were a few years older and lots of fun, walked out on the moor. We flopped down on our backs on the springy bushes that felt like a low bouncy bed covered with flowers. Bees buzzed all around but never stung us. We breathed in the fragrance of the blossoms and got drunk on the color and scent of the hills, the wildness of the moors, and the pure glory and wonder of heather.

My grandfather, Sir George Fisher-Smith—Grandpa to John and me—had died when I was five. Grandma had picked up the pieces of her life again, filled her house with guests, and plunged back into politics and charity work. She was a leader in the Liberal Party, a magistrate in the juvenile courts, which she'd helped found, and had been part of the Girl Guide movement from its earliest days. Most weekdays she was closeted in her downstairs office with Mrs. Rushworth, her secretary. We only saw her at meals and in the evenings when we and other guests gathered in the music room to dance to the player piano or play charades. The room often rocked with laughter, as when Grandma, in a shawl and pith helmet, rolled on stage in her wheelchair as Stanley looking for Livingstone.

The Gleddings brimmed with features that made life fun. Walls were crammed with paintings, chests with secret panels, and there were plenty of potted palms to hide behind. In the stone-floored kitchen with its wide hearth, Phoebe roasted meats and fowl on a hook with a brass contraption on top that rotated them slowly next to the open fire. The music room was full of Oriental and bearskin rugs, illustrated books,

The Gleddings.
Halifax.

Saturday,
Oct. 7–1922

My darling Mother—

    I must write you, even though there is only time for a note. We arrived in Halifax yesterday afternoon, Friday, October sixth, just in time for tea. Lady Fisher-Smith seemed to be awaiting our arrival, and not only kissed Francis, but kissed me too. She is very sweet—I should say about sixty years old and rather like Aunt Effie. The chauffeur came out and began bringing in our bags - Francis said to him that we did not know that we were going to stay, and he said "O! you will be here for the week-end,

TOP Letter from an American cousin describes the Gleddings in 1922.
ABOVE LEFT In fall the Conservatory overflowed with chrysanthemums.
ABOVE RIGHT Grandma loved to unlock the inlaid chest (center background) and demonstrate how it unfolded to become an ivory palace.

games, musical instruments, and paintings interspersed with stuffed heads of moose, tigers, and buffaloes that Grandpa had shot.

Best of all, there was the conservatory that smelled divinely of damp earth, geraniums, and ferns. In a sense, it was an indoor garden floored with tiles and flagstones, walled with glass, and furnished with white Alpine garden furniture that Grandma and Grandpa had picked up on their travels. In the fall there were masses of chrysanthemums in small pots—not the compact types we have today, but tall, lanky garden varieties, each one carefully staked and tied to prevent it from tumbling over. Even in the dead of winter when snow carpeted the ground outdoors, the conservatory was a magical place full of the sights and smells of spring. At Christmas there was the Christmas tree. Later in the winter, there were potted geraniums, hydrangeas, and flowering bulbs that lined the shelves or stood on the tile floor. When John and I ran through the conservatory en route to the music room, I often slowed down and lingered among the sweet-smelling plants until he came dashing back. He had to drag me away bodily to join him in some marvelous game of his invention, such as dressing up as Indians in costumes made from newspapers or draping all the Oriental rugs in the music room over the furniture to make a system of tunnels.

Grandma loved all the plants in her conservatory, especially the rose-scented geraniums. In my California garden, I grow them next to roses that have no fragrance of their own and let them tumble onto the path so that as you walk past and brush against their leaves they give fragrance to the rose. When Grandma took guests into the conservatory, she had a special comment or a story for almost every plant. The banana plant, for example, was grown in memory of how she met Grandpa. During the 1880s while taking the Grand Tour of Europe, she'd slipped on a banana peel next to the Grand Canal in Venice and fallen into his arms. Grandma repeated her stories many times and embellished them as the years went by. She always saved her most dramatic story for last, which concerned two immense blue-green century plants growing in large wooden tubs.

"These century plants from the West Coast of America are so valuable that I couldn't even begin to imagine what they're worth. You can touch them if you wish but please watch out for the spines because they're very sharp," Grandma said proudly in her striking Bostonian accent, which she never lost. "These plants came to us in a remarkable way. In 1910, when dear George and I were traveling in California, a famous plantsman gave us two tiny plants scarcely bigger than the palm of my hand. We brought them back to England and gave them to old Hubert, who was our gardener in those days. He planted them in pots, fed them, cared for them, and potted them on, until now just look at their size! But now we come to the most amazing part of this story. Century plants get their name from the fact that they live exactly one hundred years and then they die. Well, all the other century plants have already reached the age of 100 and died, so you are now looking at the very last two in the whole world!"

People gasped and stared. Grandma, who knew a great deal about politics but very little about plants, was so convincing that she even convinced herself. Then one winter day in the mid-thirties, while John and I were staying at the Gleddings and having tea with Grandma in the conservatory, a maid came in with a letter from Dad. Grandma slit open Dad's letter and read it aloud. "Dear Mother, It's raining cats and dogs out here in California," and he drew amusing pictures of them falling from the sky. The letter went on to describe his adventures in Hollywood and ended with the words, "Your loving son Emerson." Then, "P.S.—Mother dear, remember those two incredibly rare century plants in your conservatory? The ones that are the very last two in the world? Well, they must have had a great many children because out here in Hollywood they're growing all over the hillsides!"

Did Grandma mind? Not one bit. She threw back her head and laughed, and so did we. It was many years before John and I learned that century plants don't live for a hundred years, except perhaps in a European conservatory. Their actual lifespan varies from ten to thirty years, depending on soil fertility and rainfall. When they die they leave a great many progeny in the form of offshoots and seeds.

At the Gleddings there was always a steady stream of guests coming and going, including dignitaries who came to Yorkshire to give speeches— an African prince in full regalia; Lady Astor, an American like Grandma and the fastest talking woman we'd ever met; and Grey Owl, the Canadian author and Parliament member who was credited with saving the beaver from extinction. John and I had read his books and were thrilled to meet a real American Indian. His skin was brown, he wore buckskins, and his long graying hair was tied in braids. When he visited our teepee hidden among the rhododendrons, he seemed ill at ease. I now understand why: I recently bought a Penguin reprint of *Pilgrims of the Wild* and learned from the scholarly introduction that the author, Grey Owl, had actually been an Englishman masquerading as an American Indian.

When Dad was growing up at the Gleddings he had a friendship with Hubert the gardener much like John and I did with Viney. But Hubert died before we were born, and the new head gardener was unfriendly. Nonetheless, we loved the garden. When John and I arrived that August, Grandma's old moss roses, cabbage roses, and damasks were dropping their richly fragrant petals. The maids were gathering them up and spreading them out on newspapers to dry. Year-round there was a big Ming bowl full of a potpourrie of rose petals on a table at the entrance to the music room, just past the conservatory. Whenever Grandma rolled by it in her wheelchair, she reached out and took a pinch. Heads of lavender, too, were being dried the same way. Later, the maids sewed them into little bags to put among the linens and in all the drawers.

Grandma's herbaceous border was also in full bloom. It was an absolute jumble. She loved the old-fashioned flowers, such as snapdragons, foxgloves, Canterbury bells, columbines, love-in-a-mist, and phlox, so there were lots of those. But in that incongruous bed, they rubbed elbows with clunky yellow, red, and orange dahlias. The gardeners had plunked all the plants into the ground in clumps of each variety, giving no thought to arranging them by height or color or shape. I tried to pick an example of every flower in that helter-skelter bed—close to a hundred of them—and press them between sheets of blotting paper under heavy books. I dreamed of binding them into a book, finding out the name of every flower, and writing it under the dried example. But

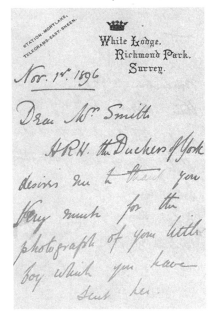

THIS DUCHESS OF YORK became Queen Mary; her husband George V knighted Grandpa.

when Grandma announced she was planning a dinner party for the following Saturday, I got sidetracked. John had one of his brain waves. He and I would produce a play for the occasion. "We'll do St. George and the Dragon," he said. "I'll be St. George, and you'll be both the princess and the dragon." We spent more time making costumes than rehearsing, which was lucky since I almost suffocated inside a gunny sack while playing the dragon. Grandma was not feeling well that week, and we didn't see much of her. On Friday, it was

THE GIRL GUIDES ASSOCIATION,
INCORPORATED BY ROYAL CHARTER.

17-19, BUCKINGHAM PALACE ROAD,

August 30th 1938   LONDON, S. W. 1.

Dear Lady Ingilby

I have just seen in "The Times" that we have lost a kind good friend to Guiding in your county ,and I feel I must write and tell you how sorry I am to hear this sad news.

I know what a great part Lady Fisher-Smith had played in the development of the Guide Movement in Halifax ,right from the earliest days of its origin,and she had always been such a generous staunch supporter to the work and its personnel.

I shall never forget how specially kind she was to the Extension .... and I see her now ,in my mind's eye ,as I .... ing a delightful party to a whole lot of .... going about amongst them and ehcouraging and .... er sympathy and kindliness .

.... Lady Fisher-Smith will be sadly missed in .... d we Guides shall always be thankful for

Yours very sincerely

Olave Baden-Powell.

LETTER OF CONDOLENCE from Lady Baden-Powell, founder of the Girl Guides (called Girl Scouts in America). Grandma was a prime mover in the Girl Guide movement. Scouts and Guides often camped in Grandma's sheep fields or on the lawns. Newspaper photo shows the event remembered in the letter.

LEFT December 1938 on the upper deck of the *Franconia*
with Dad and a friend I met on the voyage. Dad made friends with her mother,
and we all met again years later in Laguna Beach.
RIGHT Postcard of the *Franconia* I bought on board.

decided we should go back to Hoyle Court until Grandma felt better.
There would be no party on Saturday night, no St. George, no dragon.
The maids packed up our things and Alsop drove us home in the Rolls.
On Saturday morning Gran told us that Grandma had died. This was
too much for my stiff upper lip; I couldn't stop crying until they sent
for the doctor. I've never been able to recall that day or anything that
happened for the next week.

Dad took an airplane across the United States, sailed home on the
Queen Mary, and arrived in time for the funeral. One week later, he
took Harriet, Monica, John, and me for a holiday at Llandudno in
Wales to cheer us up. We stayed in a boarding house on the bay, visited
medieval castles, and built our own out of sand. We went to an island
where monks lived as they had in the Middle Ages. We learned how to
fish, catch crabs, and muddle about in boats and to know the wildflowers on the hillsides. Then John and I went back to school, but Dad
stayed on in England settling up the estate. He had a small income left
to him by Grandpa, but he had to sell most of Grandma's possessions

to settle her debts and pay her bequests.

In December, Dad listed John, Bill, and me on the quota for English immigrants to the United States. Gran came to London to see us off. Two days before Christmas of 1938, we sailed from Southhampton on the *Franconia*. Dad sailed first class; Norah, John, Bill, and I sailed tourist. Tinker, our Sealyham terrier, was in the kennel on deck. John and I spent our days with Dad. He took us on a tour of the ship, even into the steerage. We saw poor refugee families from Europe, bound for Ellis Island—men in black hats and beards, women in long dresses and kerchiefs; children of all ages. I sensed a deep sadness in the hearts of these people, even among the children. We looked at them and they at us across a gulf but united as immigrants. The old days were over, never to return.

On New Year's Day 1939, we were up before dawn and out on deck. We could barely see on the distant horizon a sliver of land. America! There we were at last, land of our hopes and dreams. Dad stood between John and me with his hands on our shoulders. With my whole heart I reached out and embraced that thin line of land. I looked forward with all my might to the adventures it would bring.

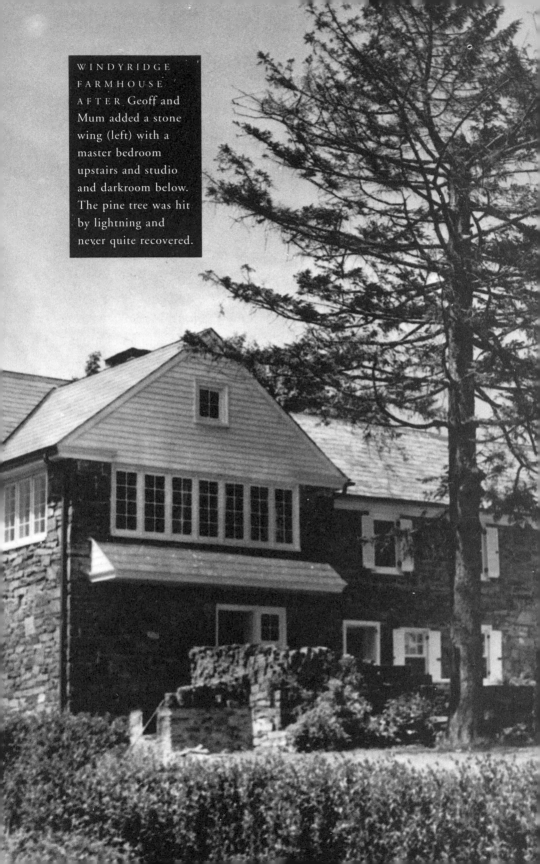

WINDYRIDGE
FARMHOUSE
AFTER Geoff and
Mum added a stone
wing (left) with a
master bedroom
upstairs and studio
and darkroom below.
The pine tree was hit
by lightning and
never quite recovered.

12.

How Mum Bought the Farm

OUR NEW LIFE in America didn't wait for us to arrive on shore. It reached out to meet the *Franconia* while we were still at sea and Dad, John, Norah, and I were watching the pilot boat come alongside. Bill was in his stroller, and I had Tinker on his leash. When the sailors dropped a ladder over the side for the pilot, Tinker went wild, broke away from me, and half ran, half slid across the deck. At that moment a tall man in a knitted sailor's cap and a navy-blue turtleneck sweater loomed up over the rail. Tinker leaped straight into his arms.

"Atta FELLA, Tinker! How now, thou noble brute!" Geoff, an old salt at heart, had talked the pilot into taking him along. He was as hearty as ever, except his Franco-Elizabethan-nautical lingo was now laced with American slang. "HI GANG!" he cried to the rest of us. "EMERSON, old chap! NORAH, old gal! And GOSSE! How was thy crossing, eh?—Were ye landlubbers SEASICK? Told your mother t'would be bound to happen. And hi to THEE, son Bill!" Geoff stuck his grinning mustachioed face into Bill's. Bill howled. "Not used to your old Pop yet, eh, fella-mi-lad?"

He turned his back to the wind, pulled his pipe out of his pocket, and began stuffing it with tobacco. We hadn't expected to be reunited with Geoff so soon; it was Mum we most wanted to see, but Tinker was ecstatic. We steamed into New York harbor and passed the Statue of Liberty. At dockside, Mum was waiting for us with open arms. At first, Bill didn't recognize her. He howled when she reached to pick him up, but Mum made a joke of it. "If my mother had taken off half-way round the world, I wouldn't remember her either!"

It took some time for us all to become readjusted. I felt awkward and unnatural, and John's face twitched, as it sometimes did when he was nervous. Norah was stiff and disapproving. She'd always loved Mum and Dad, but disliked Geoff. "Guess what!" said Mum, who had anticipated everything. "We're going to go to a real American drugstore and have coffee ice-cream sodas—something you never had in England. You too, Emerson!" But Dad couldn't stay to smooth things over. He had to catch a train. He hugged us good-bye, shook hands with Geoff, kissed Mum, and disappeared into the crowd. He'd promised John and me that he would see us soon. "I'm going to leave Hollywood and move east," he'd told us.

After the sodas had had their mollifying effect, Geoff drove us to Long Island in their secondhand Buick sedan, the most streamlined car John or I had ever seen. I sat in the back with my nose glued to the window looking for a glimpse of cactus, sagebrush, or at least a cottonwood tree. I knew about New York City, the Empire State Building, and the lakes, rivers, and hardwood forests of the East Coast, but I'd seen too many cowboy movies. With a total lack of logic I expected the Old West too. It was several weeks before I realized that the Lone Ranger and his countryside weren't to be found here or anywhere, for that matter, but that someday I might encounter a newer version of them two thousand miles further west.

As soon as we arrived at the woodsy house Mum and Geoff had rented near the Long Island Sound in Huntington Beach, Geoff suggested we look around the garden. First things first in this family! Geoff had already started a compost pile out of grass clippings and fallen leaves. He proudly turned a forkful over and a cloud of steam rose into the frosty air.

"We're going to make a vegetable garden right here," he gestured and John and I laughed. The house was on the edge of a wooded ravine, and the place Geoff had chosen for his garden was under a fallen tree. "Oh THAT," he shrugged as if it were a matchstick. "Well, naturally we'll have to saw up yon log first and chop it into firewood. That's our winter's work, and you gosse are going to help! A wingdinger of a hurricane CHARGED through here last summer, uprooted that tree and many another. RIGHT-O CHAPS! Indoors now!"

Meanwhile, Mum had lit a crackling fire in the fireplace. At the far end of the room there was a Christmas tree and a pile of packages— woolen snowsuits, knee-high leather boots, and red woolen socks for each of us, including Norah; toys for Bill, and ice skates and Flexible Flyer sleds for John and me. We had not expected Christmas, especially on New Year's Day.

Never in the whole time we lived on the East Coast did we again enjoy such great sledding and skating as during that winter of 1939. Mum enrolled us both in public schools. John did well, but I was behind in math and found it difficult to make friends. It was bad enough having an English accent, but Norah had sent me to school on the first day dressed in my best tweed coat and its matching hat with little velvet-lined cat's ears. After that gaffe, I spent my free time building a dugout in the woods with John and neighborhood boys or sitting on the roof of the woodshed devouring *Uncle Tom's Cabin, Anne of Green Gables, Rebecca of Sunnybrook Farm,* and other American books suggested by Miss Palmer, my kind-hearted teacher. She behaved towards me like a conscientious gardener towards a fresh transplant, solicitously pouring fertilizer around its roots.

In a month or two Norah sailed back to England. The morning after Norah left, John knocked on Mum's and Geoff's bedroom door and asked, "What shall I wear?" "What do you mean what shall you wear?" cried Mum. "Go look in your closet, pick something out, and put it on!" John, who'd been raised to be an English squire and had always had his clothes laid out for him, raised one eyebrow at Mum and stalked off down the hall. From now on we were meant to fend for ourselves. There followed a stream of hired help who couldn't manage Bill and didn't fit in with the family. Then one auspicious day a pleasant, strong-looking young woman with wavy blond hair rang our doorbell and applied for the job.

"How old are you?" asked Mum.

"Eighteen and just graduated from Oyster Bay High School. My mother died and I live with my dad, but he and I don't get along. I can cook and do housework. I'm used to children, I'm good natured, I'm hard working, and willing to do anything."

"You're hired!" said Mum.

From the very first moment, Irene fitted in. She loved all of us, understood Bill, helped me with math, had a great sense of humor, and hit it off with Mum as if they were lifelong friends. Their laughter resounded through the house, but soon after Irene arrived, Mum became depressed. She'd gotten used to working with Geoff and couldn't adjust to staying home and taking care of three young children, even with Irene to help. Furthermore, she was lying awake nights worrying about money. Then one day the solution to her dilemma popped into her head. She could hardly wait until Geoff came home that evening. As soon as they were alone in front of the fire she poured out her heart. Though I didn't hear the conversation, years later Mum told me the gist of it.

"I want to buy a farm and run it like a business," Mum said. "It'll be our war effort! It will help us out financially, and farms are wonderful places for bringing up children. Oh, Geoff, I'm so excited about the idea! Father had a farm, so I actually know something about it. I love animals. I love plants. I love fixing up houses. I know I can do it!"

"Sold!" said Geoff. "When do we start to look?"

"This weekend!" laughed Mum. And they did.

Geoff brought home a map of the East Coast and drew concentric circles around New York City. "We'll start looking inside the circle closest to New York and then move farther out." Every weekend after that, Mum and Geoff went farm hunting. They drove hundreds of miles on back roads in Connecticut, New Jersey, and New York and looked at dozens of farms. They knew what they wanted—sturdy buildings, a pleasant setting, a reliable water supply, and above all fertile soil so we could raise crops as well as animals. But every farm they looked at was either too expensive or too run down.

"Why don't you come and spend the weekend with us on our farm in Bucks County, Pennsylvania?" Jean Spadea suggested. "Perhaps you can find something round there. After all, we did." Following Mum's meeting with the Spadeas on the *Georgic* in 1937, the two couples had become firm friends and occasional business associates.

"Too far out," said Geoff.

"Oh, come on!" urged Jim. "Loosen up. Take a break. It will do Ruth good. You too if you let it."

The Spadea's farm wouldn't have fitted our needs. The barn was pictureque but somewhat delapitated, and the land was best-adapted to running sheep. But there was an excellent well, and the house was delightful. A wide front porch overlooked a wild and lovely garden with a wide grassy path that lead through a meadow down to a flagstone-edged swimming pool. Jim was ahead of his time. He did all the cooking, the gardening, and

JIM AND JEAN SPADEA (shown here in 1954) were important figures in the New York fashion world, as well as Mum and Geoff's best friends.

the housework; he even raised the kids. Jean was two personas, both elegant. At the office she was all business, tossing orders right and left and shaking finished designs out of her sleeve onto the drawing board, but in the country, she was languid, vague, and devastatingly charming.

On their farm Jim grew zucchinis, eggplants, tomatoes, and lashings of basil as well as flowers. He kept goats for their milk. He grew grapes over an arbor that shaded the back terrace, just like in Italy, and served up his red wine and ratatouille on a red-checkered table cloth at a long dining table under the arbor. As the years went by, we met many of the writers in Bucks County around that table, but on that first weekend before the war Mum and Geoff were concentrating more on their project than the other guests. They fell in love with the Spadea's farm and Bucks County—it reminded them of England. Two weekends later, they found our farm.

The property was near Doylestown, not far from the Spadeas. The buildings faced south across a tranquil valley. A stream ran through the bottom of it, and woods rose up the hill on the other side. The sturdy L-shaped stone house had a clapboard addition that made it into a T. The original stone part dated from the eighteenth century. The house needed a new furnace and modern plumbing. The roof leaked, the woodwork needed painting or scraping, and there were partitions to remove. But its beams, doors, windowsills, floors, and shutters were sound, its cellar dry.

It had a lovely view and was shaded by mature trees—several maples, a plum, a pear, and a weeping willow. The farm buildings were in better shape than the house—solid corn crib and outhouses, old stone spring house, stone ice house, and a huge new barn with a silo; the original barn had burned down. There were fifty acres of land, two streams, two orchards, two pastures, a wood, and six gently-sloping fields divided by hedge-rows almost like English ones. Above all, the soil was fertile red clay with some rocks in it to make it drain well.

LATE WINTER 1939, Mum attacks a tree felled by 1938 hurricane.

Geoff and Mum didn't go on instinct alone; they asked the opinion of the County Agent, the state and federal farm advisor. He agreed the farm was a good buy, and confirmed their belief that the soil was fertile. He also told Mum and Geoff they'd have good neighbors, the Hovsepians, a fine Armenian family with a truck route in Philadelphia, who lived on the hill to the east. The family included four grown sons who could help us plow and plant and teach us how to milk our cows. The County Agent, according to Mum, acted as if he had little faith in this young Englishwoman's ability to run a farm. "Are you sure you know what you're getting into?" he asked. And Mum replied, "You'll see!" He had challenged her, and she made up her mind to show him.

Before Mum and Geoff left the farm that early-summer day, a gust of wind rustled the leaves in the maple trees. Mum said, "Let's call it Windyridge Farm." It cost her nine thousand dollars, all the money she had left in the nest egg she'd brought over from England. When Geoff and Mum came home that night, they were ecstatic, though Mum was afraid Irene wouldn't want to move so far from home. But Irene surprised her by announcing, "I've always wanted to live on a farm!"

Mum had a conference with John and me to let us know what she expected from us. "The place needs a lot of fixing up," she said, "but we'll take out a mortgage and do most of the work ourselves. Farm life is wonderful, but it's not all fun and games. We must all work together. You children will have to do your share, except for Bill; he's too young. We'll move this summer."

John and I relished the idea of living on a farm, but just then Dad swooped down out of nowhere, as he had a habit of doing. He was still single; he had not yet met Margot. He said, "Ruth, you're biting off more than you can chew. I'll take John and Pat off your hands for a year. You'll have fewer mouths to feed, and only one child to bother with." What! Us a bother? John and I were shocked. We were such polite, well-behaved children—we thought—the kind who never ever annoyed adults by getting in their hair. Nonetheless, we were quite happy to pack up and go with Dad, because what he proposed sounded like fun. "I've rented a house in Nyack, New York," he told us. "You'll love it, but I've sublet it for the summer. We're going to spend the summer in Maine!" Thanks to Miss Palmer, I already knew and loved Maine. I'd been there in my imagination while reading *Rebecca of Sunnybrook Farm.*

13.

How Dad Turned Us into Americans

EVERYWHERE WE WENT en route north, we were welcomed with open arms by our New England cousins, uncles, and aunts in much the same way that Grandma had once welcomed so many of them when they'd traveled to England and visited the Gleddings. Dad played the court jester in every house, and everyone adored him. His favorite after-dinner act was a take-off on Adolf Hitler. He smarmed his black hair over his left forehead, blackened his upper lip, and spat out a speech in bogus German escalating to a crazy finale of frenzied rage.

Dad was artistic. That summer he and I began painting watercolors together, sitting side-by-side, silent, and absorbed. He was also incredibly absent minded, like Aunt Elizabeth,

MARGOT SNORKELING IN the Mediterranean on one of Dad's linoleum-block Christmas cards.

JOHN AND I on a canoe trip with Dad at Lake Allamoosook, Maine in the summer of 1939.

the subject of his most amusing stories. Dad loved us—I always felt safe with Dad—but John and I also got the impression that we had to take care of him. We wondered how he ever managed without us. He was constantly losing his paint brushes, his pocket calendar, his wallet, or his glasses. He had a habit of accidentally pouring cream into his grapefruit. He would often don socks that didn't match, and if we didn't watch out, he would forget he was in America and start driving on the left. In Dad's old age, he and Margot built a little villa on the island of Malta with nothing but wild rosemary and rockroses between them and the Mediterranean. There, he gave up trying to remember which side of the road to drive on and settled on the middle. "Crazy Maltese!" he'd yell after barely missing the car of a terrified oncoming driver.

Despite the hazards of the road, we arrived safely in the state of Maine and stopped at L.L. Bean where Dad outfitted us in jeans, red flannel shirts, sweatshirts, mocassins, slickers, and gum boots. We spent July in a cabin at Lake Alamoosook, where cousin Eleanor French owned a children's summer camp on an island in the middle of the lake. This is where Dad's competent side showed itself. He'd learned the art of woodcraft as a boy, and he'd never forgotten it. He often said he was Peter Pan, a boy who never grew up. In Maine he taught us how to canoe, camp in the wilds, and cook the fish we caught over a campfire. He managed our fishing tackle with deft fingers, kept all the parts of it neat and clean, and knew the spots where the trout were rising. We saw beaver and kingfishers and wild rice growing at the water's edge. I was in heaven. I felt as though I'd stepped right into the pages of a book by my then-favorite writer, Ernest Thompson Seton. At last, in August, we went to Pond Island.

Some of the best stories our grandmother, Lady Hattie Fisher-Smith, had told us in the old days at the Gleddings had been about Pond Island, a real family island owned by the Campbell Clan in Narraguagus Bay, five miles off the coast from Milbridge in Down East Maine, the northeast coastal section. (Grandma's mother was a Campbell.) For hundreds of years, the Indians had kept this and many other islands burned off to encourage birds to nest so they could collect their eggs. In the seventeenth and eighteenth centuries, Europeans, seeing the islands needed no clearing, settled them first. One family settled on Pond Island and grew potatoes. Trading ships loaded with goods sailed north from Boston, following the coastline. When the Maine coast turned and jutted out to sea, the ships that were skirting it sailed due east, the off-shore breeze behind them. They hoisted all their canvas and sailed before the wind. It was "down wind all the way," hence the term "Down East Maine." After the trading ships emptied their cargoes in northern ports, they had to tack back against the wind. In sheltered bays near islands such as Pond Island, they stopped to fill their empty hulls with a ballast of round beach rocks and to load up with sacks of potatoes to sell in Boston. In Boston harbor, they unloaded the potatoes and the rocks. The potatoes went into New England chowders; the round rocks cobbled Boston's roads.

By the last half of the nineteenth century, the sailing ships had long since stopped coming, the thin soil was farmed out, and Pond Island was up for sale. On July 17, 1876, two of Grandma's uncles, Fred and David Campbell, and two distant relations of theirs bought the island for a song as a place to spend the summer holidays with their families.

T O P When we arrived at the Pond Island landing, we didn't know what to expect.
A B O V E John and I in the lobsterman's boat en route to Pond Island, still
looking like very English children.
O P P O S I T E The abandoned lighthouse on Pond Island in the background
above the Devil's Punch Bowl.

A year or two later, they built a big wooden house on the island with a porch down one side and a cupola on top. Grandma and Grandpa had often sailed across the Atlantic from England to spend the month of August there. But even Grandma's glowing descriptions of Pond Island and the photographs I'd seen of it from the earliest days hadn't prepared me for how wonderful that island actually was.

When Dad and John and I arrived in Russell Turner's boat—Russell was the local lobsterman—a whole group of cousins, including a number of children, were waiting onshore. For the rest of that summer, we children were all over Pond Island, on top of it, around it, and underneath it. We were in and out of every cove. We explored its every nook and cranny, and even rafted to nearby Turkey Island where we got stuck and had to be rescued by boat.

Pond Island is a mile long and three-quarters of a mile across, with a Devil's Punch Bowl, a Thunder Gulch, and an abandoned lighthouse at one end. It also has a rough-and-ready golf course, a spooky swamp, a boat landing, and a pond at the other end. The lighthouse end is clad with a dark and mossy spruce forest in the midst of which stands a two-hundred-foot high hill, called "the mountain." On a clear day in the thirties and forties you could see Mount Desert Island from the top of it. The last time I was up there—in 1972—the trees had grown too tall. There was, and still is, a cairn on the summit. Tradition dictates that everyone who climbs the mountain has to add a rock to it.

On the windward shore where winter storms had buffeted the bank above the rocks, we hunted for arrowheads and sometimes found one. There were stories of buried treasure, but no one ever dug. Sheep ran on the island and kept the paths

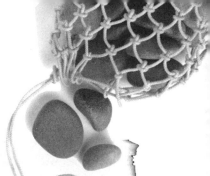

POND ISLAND

1 We arrived yesterday here on Pond Island which is
up on the coast of Maine. It is about three or four
miles round and one or two miles long, but that is only
what I think and it may be wrong. John and I have never
been here before so we did not think it would be nearly as nice as it is. We came over in the motor boat from
the main land. One of our cousins was getting his lobsters from the lobster man. I think his name is Cousin
Michael but I am not sure. Anyway, he greeted us warmly.
Then dad said to us there was an old truck on the island
so John and I ran to get to the main house to get it.
Cousin Bess told us who to get to drive it so we got the
man to drive it and he drove it down to the beach and got
our luggage. We drove in the back. After the ride in
the truck we went to our bungalow and chose our rooms.
made the bed and swept the carpet and so on. We went to
the big house and were introduced to Cousin Loren, who
is in his twenties, and Marianna, aged fourteen and
Joanne, aged seven. That evening we all five of us went
to climb on the rocks and we saw the Thunder Gulch and
the Devil's Punch Bowl and all of us were late for supper.

2 When I woke up this morning I did n't know where Iwas.
But in a second I remembered and looked at my clock. It
saidtwenty four minutes past seven so I waited till half
past seven then I woke up Dad and John, for breakfast is
at eight. So we dressed and went across the field to
breakfast. After breakfast I did the washing and John
made a raft and in the afternoon we bathed and then explored. It was lovely going through the tangled forest
and climbing over big branches and rocks, rocks then
woods, hills then dales. We climbed until we thought it
time to go back for supper and I must say I slept likea
top.

3 Last night I wrote of the day we came which was the
day before yesterday and our first day on the island which
was yesterday. But tonight I will tell you of today, but
something that I ought to have told you before is that
Pond Island is a family island and that everybody is
cousin if not uncle or aunt to everybody else. Well,
this morning we got up and went to breakfast and after
that we went up the mountain which is a hill and being

OPPOSITE The author in kids' heaven, already well-soaked above the knee
perhaps from slipping on seaweed and falling into a tidepool. John is already
two coves ahead.

ABOVE My 1939 Pond Island diary. Aunt Bess typed it so I could read it
aloud as after-dinner entertainment.

TOP A lobsterman's bait bag I found on the beach and filled with pebbles.

open and the golf course roughly clipped. One of the things we children were supposed to do that summer, besides slicing beans and shelling peas, was to pull up small seedling spruce trees that sprouted in the golf course. It was a type of gardening. The forest would soon take back the island if we didn't hold it back. The sheep kept many native plants from growing, but the family had acquired five other islands in the same archipelago and, gradually and quite casually, eleven others stretching all the way to Mount Desert Island. These were kept pristine as nature made them.

In cousin Charles and Frances Carey's beautiful all-wooden sloop, *Foggy*, we sailed to one of those wild islands and found it so thick with undergrowth and bracken you couldn't walk across it. Beach pea and beachhead iris bloomed above the cobbled beach, huckleberries and cranberries grew on the edge of the woods, a Swainson's thrush sang once from cover, and an osprey wheeled overhead. On the mud flat on the leeward side, we dug a bucketful of clams to take back to Pond Island, soak in water with a handful of cornmeal in it to remove the sand, and then steam and eat with butter. Sailing home, with my pockets filled with lovely rocks—different from Pond Island ones—while following John to the bow, I accidentally let go of the rail and fell overboard. The water off the coast of Maine is like ice, and everyone feared I'd drown. I was saved by my L.L. Bean sweater, slicker, and gum boots, and a layer of fat, recently augmented with doughnut holes rolled in sugar and served hot through the kitchen window of the Big House by Mrs. Turner, the lobsterman's wife.

Dad, John, and I stayed in cousin Henrietta's camp, one of a handful of cottages built in addition to the Big House. For breakfast, lunch, and dinner, we walked across the meadow and joined cousins from all over the United States and several parts of the world to dine on benches at long tables in the dining room of the Big House. In the huge kitchen with its iron stove, Mrs. Turner cooked soul-satisfying, Down East food: blueberry cakes and doughnuts—the holes were just a between-meals snack—fish chowder, baked beans, steamed clams, and for special occasions, boiled lobster with melted butter. We always cooked and ate the clams and lobsters on the beach. There were games and skits after dinner. Dad did his Hitler impersonation, and everyone played charades. People improvised with seaweed and bathing caps; a favorite costume was an old plaid cape of Grandma's that still hung in the upstairs hall.

We hated to leave Pond Island, but it was time to go back to school. The tiny pre-Revolutionary house that Dad had rented in Nyack in New York state was not a disappointment; it was part stone, part wood, loaded with charm, and hidden behind a tall lilac hedge with an apple orchard at one end and a vegetable garden still giving crops on the other. We had our own squash, gourds, Indian corn, herbs, rows of everlasting flowers, and tiny red and yellow tomatoes to eat straight from the vine. There were three bedrooms upstairs and a dining room and kitchen downstairs with a narrow staircase that wound straight down into the kitchen. Dad was an enthusiastic cook and could concoct a gourmet dish out of a chicken, a can of peas, a can of tomatoes, a splash of red wine, and a handful of herbs. He amused John and me enormously by his antics, such as tasting a spoonful of cocktail sauce before reading the label that said to be sure to dilute it first. My bedroom under the eaves had a dormer window that touched the floor. One night I discovered I could lie in bed and gaze down on the vegetable garden flooded with the autumn moon.

The next morning, John had another of his brain waves. "I'm going to jump out of your bedroom window," he said, "and walk in through the front door. Dad'll be so surprised! He won't know how I got there." I could hear Dad rattling around in the kitchen beneath my bedroom and smell the aroma of bacon sizzling in the pan, but John's idea sounded like fun. A shaggy lawn sloped up from the vegetable garden to the stone wall of the house. It didn't look far down. "Okay," I said, "but I'm coming, too." John eased his body out of the window, and leaped outward with catlike grace. When I tried it, I hung straight down by my fingertips and simply let go. I landed next to the wall, banged my knees against it and let out a howl. Poor Dad came running out of the house. Like Grandma years ago, he was surprised but not in the way John had anticipated.

Dad enrolled us in Nyack's public schools. Despite the fact that England and France had just declared war on Germany and times were pretty grim, he settled down to giving parties, meeting girls, and having a good time. We woke up one Sunday morning and found half-filled glasses all over the living room and Dad in bed between the twin sisters of one of his closest friends. "Jeanie and Janey were too tiddley to drive home last night," he mumbled. "Couldn't let them. Might have landed in the ditch, you know."

A few days later Dad asked me, "Are you happy in your school?"

"It's all right," I answered.

"Just as I thought; you hate it. I know a school you'll like much better. We're going to move."

"Move!" I said. "Again? Where are we going?"

"Florida."

We packed in a tremendous rush and left Nyack before dawn. "I was going to have to marry one or the other of those twins and I just couldn't make up my mind," said Dad. Now here was something else we really needed to be doing—protecting him from women. "First stop, Windyridge Farm. I've phoned your mother and said we should arrive in time for lunch."

Geoff was driving a brand new tractor into the barn as Dad lurched his bottle-green convertible out of a rut, turned off Stump Road, and drove down the gravel drive. Mum was eager to show us the house. She and Irene had been painting walls, scraping doors, and apparently having a great time. "We're going room by room," she laughed, "and keeping the other doors closed so we don't get discouraged. I feel like a pioneer woman."

There were workmen everywhere. A plumber was connecting drains. Our three-year-old brother Bill was following an electrician around and saying "What's that?" every time he picked up a tool. Two carpenters were fitting a heavy oak door between the kitchen and the living room and soundproofing its edges with thick felt pads. "ALORS, les mecs! C'est FORMIDAAABLE!" cried Geoff to the carpenters, as if they'd just stepped off a ship from France. Then he turned to us. "After these good chaps have finished, you gosse will be able to hoot your heads off in the kitchen, see? Your mother and I will be able to have our fireside chats in the living room, and it'll be peaceful as a bloody millpond!"

We stayed long enough for lunch and to see the farm buildings, the remains of the vegetable garden, and the double row of raspberries Geoff had already planted, then it was time to go. We had a long drive ahead of us, said Dad, and many cousins to visit en route south. Dad's idea of travel was not to miss the points of interest as you went along, so while we were staying with our cousins, we also saw the monuments and museums of Washington, D.C.

When we left Nyack I was sleeping under two blankets at night and kicking a carpet of orange and golden leaves on the way to school, but soon we caught up with summer again, threw the blankets off our beds, and rolled down all the windows of the car. The three of us sat in a row in Dad's little convertible; it had no backseat. I sat by the window, gazing out of it and enjoying every minute. Dad drove, and John sat in the middle reading the map. When we came to a fork in the road, they argued about which way to go; John was usually right. We rarely saw another car. Along with the change in climate came a new and exotic set of plants, species I'd never seen before except in books. Equally exotic to me was the sight of large black families, people like those I'd read about in *Uncle Tom's Cabin*, working side-by-side in fields of cotton or sitting on the front porches of ramshackle shacks next to the two-lane road.

We passed mansions with pillars on the front that could have used several Mums and Irenes with buckets of paint and a whole slew of carpenters. We rolled across mile after dull flat mile of turpentine pines and past live oaks dripping with Spanish moss. We stopped to visit historic places, and then at last we saw palm trees! To me this was Tarzan country—he was another of my secret loves. It wasn't Africa exactly, but close enough.

We settled in Daytona Beach, a bit too civilized for Tarzan, but I discounted that, read every Tarzan book in the local library, and imagined him swinging from every tree. The gardens overflowed with oleanders, petunias, and palmettos; perfume wafted on the breeze. Dad rented the bottom floor of a house two blocks from the beach. The upstairs was rented by a divorced writer named Mrs. West and her three sons with whom John and I played Monopoly on rainy days. Dad and Mrs. West had one date, but Dad's car had gotten stuck in a sand dune en route to the hard-packed, coquina-shell beach. They trailed home in single file at dawn, barefoot, in their evening clothes, carrying their shoes, and never spoke to each other again.

We were a block or two from cousin Henrietta's winter house—the same cousin who'd lent us her Pond Island cottage—and two blocks from the home of Dr. and Mrs. Wood, close friends Dad had met on a cruise. Their daughter Mary was just a few months older than me and the most popular girl in our school. The minute we met, she became my "bosom friend," just like I'd read about in *Anne of Green Gables*. Mary once told me she always looked back on that year as the best period of her childhood. Most of the other girls in the fifth grade were even more unfriendly than the children in Nyack and Long Island. Years later

TOP The palm trees and jungle atmosphere of exotic spots like Juniper
Springs, Florida, changed the focus of my imagination from Indians to Tarzan.
LEFT Dad's bottle-green convertible got us safely to Florida despite battle
scars. The three of us sat in the front, John in the middle reading the map and
me on the far right with my nose glued to the window.
RIGHT Seeing palm trees for the first time was exciting for two kids who'd
left the shores of England less than a year before.

Dad explained their reaction. "A lot of people were prejudiced against the English," he said. "They thought England had dragged the United States into World War I, and they were afraid it might happen again."

In those days—the late thirties and early forties—Florida was largely unspoiled. Deserted beaches stretched for miles, and Dad took John and me on adventurous trips. We took a boat deep into the Everglades, and a troupe of wild monkeys, escapees from a zoo, jumped aboard. We grabbed our seat cushions and helped the boatman beat them off. We saw alligators in the wild, ate frogs legs, and watched Seminole Indians weave baskets. Wearing face masks, we dove into a crystal-clear spring and swam across the center of it. We could see straight down, fifty feet or more, to where the water bubbled up from the base of the spring, shaped like an inverted cone.

In Florida Dad gave up cooking and hired a large black lady, Geneva, who was sweet but sad, arrived before breakfast, left after dinner, kept the house sparkling, and cooked like an angel. When he wasn't traveling with John and me, Dad spent his time playing tennis, going to parties, and chasing girls. He soon gave up chasing all of them at once and concentrated on one, Margot Gould; she was blond, beautiful, and twenty-eight years old. Dad was forty-five. At first John and I tried to protect Dad from her. I can imagine what a hit this made with Margot, but she won. Before the winter season was over and the hotel closed for the summer, they were engaged.

By the time school was out, most winter vacationers had long since left Florida. Dad, John, and I were glad when we too could leave the steaming heat behind us and drive north to Windyridge Farm. "Let me look at you!" cried Mum, when we arrived. "Several inches taller and brown as berries. I'll have to admit your father's turned you into a couple of real Americans."

14.

How Mum Made Us into Farmers

A FEW YEARS AGO, when I was having dinner with several members of the Garden Writers of America, I stumbled across the secret ingredient that turns an ordinary gardener into a garden writer—chicken manure. Each of us had, at one time or another, lived on a chicken farm. Now, if you've ever lived on a chicken farm you know that nothing, absolutely nothing, makes things grow quite as rapidly as chicken manure. People who have grown a garden with its aid are bound to think they can grow anything and should devote their lives to telling others how.

When John and I reached Windyridge Farm, we soon discovered it contained a bonanza of chicken manure in the form of an enormous and evil-smelling heap, spilling over from the manure spreader on the far side of the barn. Geoff zealously spread the stuff on the ground. In response, every green thing on our fifty acres of good ground grew. A person could actually talk himself into liking the smell of horse or cow manure, as Geoff evidently had done prior to spreading one or the other on his beloved raspberries with the cheery chant, "Oh thou yummy CAVIAR for plants—HEAVE-HO! Rot merrily on yon ground. Hey, nonny-non." But chicken manure is grey and white, shiney, wet, gooey, gunky stuff that never loses its disgusting smell. Shortly after my arrival at Windyridge Farm, I discovered that I was about to become an expert in the scientific disposal of this product. In other words, one of my major jobs was to clean off the chicken roosts in the barn.

Windyridge Farm was indeed just as Mum had said it would be, a wonderful life, great for children but also a lot of work. In an article Mum wrote for *Vogue* magazine in 1942, she breezily said the children—John and I, that is—hadn't worked much in the beginning. This lasted about a week. For the first days, Mum gave us a few light chores such as collecting eggs, harvesting vegetables, and feeding the calf and pigs. The rest of the time we were free to explore the farm and get acquainted with the Hovsepians. After that, it became clear that we, too, should put our shoulders to the wheel. As Mum said, "Many hands make light work." She was full of homilies picked up in Yorkshire— "Least said, soonest mended," when John and I had had a fight; "What they don't know won't hurt them," after Geoff dropped a steak on the kitchen floor while the guests were in the garden, and "It's an ill wind that blows no good," when we ran out of hay, rigged a floodlight in the

MUM'S CHICKENS WERE
a great source of money and manure.

barn, and roller skated on the smooth floor of the hayloft.

Mum had a habit of giving everyone and everything a label. Irene was a "farmerette" and she was a "pioneer woman," but our label for Mum was "five-star general." The rest of us were "her troops." Irene and the numerous carpenters, plumbers, and electricians who tripped over each other in house and barn were the "commissioned officers." Various hired men and women who couldn't hold a candle to Irene were the "reserve forces" who drifted in and out. And down on the bottom two rungs of the ladder of command were "Sergeant John" and "Private Pat." Bill was only four years old, and spent his time following the troops and asking questions. Just where Geoff fitted into this hierachy is a bit unclear since he was in New York all week and only came home on weekends. Perhaps he was the President; as time went by he often countermanded the plans of the general and substituted those of his own.

Mum ran the farm by "the Book," a ten-volume encyclopedia of farming that she'd invested in along with the farm. She also consulted stacks of government pamphlets. Every weeknight after dinner, while Irene, John, and I did the dishes and made a hullabaloo on the other side of the soundproofed door, Mum went to her desk in the living room and studied the Book and all those pamphlets. The next morning she mustered her troops and told us all what to do. Monday mornings were special. That was when Mum handed out her "little lists" of jobs for the week, headed "PAT—TO DO," "JOHN—TO DO," and "IRENE—TO DO." She even made one for herself—"RUTH—TO DO." When Geoff was home he got one, too. More often than not, John and I found our lists included "Scrape manure off chicken roosts."

Mum and Geoff had built a three-storey chicken house inside the barn, facing the windows away from Stump Road to preserve the barn's facade. The north end of the barn remained an open loft for straw, hay, feed, and farm equipment. Next, they converted the former chicken

THE BROODER HOUSE and barn after Mum and Geoff had converted them to raise chickens. The large, square hole in the wall was for the manure chute.

house into a two-room brooder house with 250 baby chicks tweeting away under each brooder. Mum chose Rhode Island Reds because they were good for eggs as well as eating and smarter than white Leghorns. "Leghorns lay more eggs per chicken," said Mum, "but they peck each other to death when they're chicks, and the pullets roost in trees. You have to chase them down before you can lock them into the range houses to protect them from foxes."

By the time John and I arrived, Mum and Irene had raised a flock of 300 lovely fat laying hens who clucked away contentedly in the barn. They had an additional few hundred cockerels out to range to sell as broilers. In a year or two, when the operation reached its peak, we had a total of 2,500 chickens, and Mum was already making the farm pay. Her crate of eggs commanded a fancy price at the weekly auction in Doylestown, and her dressed chickens sold directly to restaurants and hotels. The County Agent often dropped by to give advice. By now, Mum had completely won him over. When there was an outbreak of chicken pox, he arrived with the vet and we all stayed up all night inoculating every single chicken on the farm.

The first time John and my TO DO lists included "Scrape manure off chicken roosts" my reaction was "Ugh!," but it was only a fleeting thought. One didn't complain to Mum. If one did she'd reply, "Buck up now! Where's your spirit?" or look at you searchingly and say, "That doesn't sound like you! Are you feeling all right?" On our farm even the chickens were cooperative, not the disobedient kind like those Betty McDonald described in her book, *The Egg and I*—but of course they were Leghorns so what could anyone expect? Once Mum had instructed John and me on the general principles of barn cleanliness and scientific manure disposal, or anything else for that matter, she left us entirely alone to figure out how to do it. John's predilection for brain waves came in very handy on the farm.

Each floor of the chicken house contained a large steel manure hopper hanging from a metal track. All you had to do was wait until the chickens were inside their laying boxes and then wheel the manure hopper smoothly along on its track beside the roosts and pull the manure with a long-handled scraper from the galvanized pans on the table under the roosts straight into the hopper. When you reached the end of the line you hoisted one side of the hopper and scraped the manure into a shoot that sent it out a square window in the wall straight onto the manure spreader standing behind the barn. If you dawdled the job could take all day.

John suggested that by working together and racing each other we could quickly pile the manure into a heap under each roost. Then he would ride on the back of the hopper kicking it along with one foot while I ran ahead and shoved each pile quickly into the hopper's mouth as it went roaring by. Faster and faster we went, I making up silly chants about manure and sending it flying and John whistling like a train and skidding the hopper around on the track. At the end of the line it hit the wall—CLANG!—and tipped over, jettisoning the manure into the shoot, out the window, hopefully onto the spreader below. The chickens cackled loudly and out plopped their eggs. We finished the job at least an hour early and spent the stolen time climbing up the barn's ladders and jumping into the hay mound.

During the long, cold winter, while Dad, John, and I were basking in the warmth of Florida and swimming in the turquoise sea, Mum and Irene had scraped all the paint from all the woodwork in the farmhouse and then waxed it to bring out the natural beauty of the old pine. They'd stripped the walls of wallpaper and painted all the ceilings and walls, sewn bedspreads for every bed and curtains for every window, and furnished the downstairs rooms with oak antiques we'd brought from England. When spring arrived they toured the countryside for

OPPOSITE Farm kids usually learn to drive the tractor and work with other farm machinery at an early age. We were no exception.

ABOVE Though Bill was too young to work he loved farm life as much as the rest of us.

TOP RIGHT Irene with Dawn, our first cow, who thought she was a dog.

BOTTOM RIGHT Even with a paint brush in her hand, Mum always looked as if she'd stepped out of the pages of a fashion magazine.

GEOFF PHOTOGRAPHING
MODELS against our barn door with
one of the silos in the background. The
back of this photo says "This is my
stepfather Geoff—he's wonderfull" (*sic*).

bedroom furniture. "We bought queer objects from junk shops and barns," wrote Mum in her article for *Vogue*. "We fell on them with lye and scrubbing brushes, scraped them down to the bare wood, and then waxed until our arms ached." What's more, Mum—the former socialite who used to ride to the hounds, drive fast cars, and yacht around Scotland—considered this period "the most soul-satisfying time I have ever had in my life."

Meanwhile, working on weekends, Geoff plowed and manured the fields, planted them with corn and alfalfa, and put in a huge vegetable garden. "My husband is a born gardener," wrote Mum, "and everything came up in such unexpected quantities, in fact, that I had to start canning right away. I read all the canning literature I could, bought a pressure cooker, and started in." Mum and Irene loved it and I did too when I'd arrived from Florida. We were all swept up in Mum's enthusiasm. Many times we had an assembly line, with me picking the beans, Irene putting them through the slicer, and Mum canning. We sang, joked, and laughed as we worked. Sometimes we raced each other to shell a collander of peas, slip the skins off a peck of blanched tomatoes, or French-cut a bushel of beans. A year later we got a deep freezer; it was quicker than canning and we got a better-tasting product. But Mum made all the jam herself the old-fashioned way in small batches—four cups of fruit to three cups of sugar boiled quickly over a hot stove—and her "Last of Garden" mustard pickles from an old English recipe were divine.

On top of all the canning, freezing, pickling, and jamming, Mum, Irene, and I did the wash every Monday, put it through the mangle, and hung it out on lines on the front lawn. We ironed on Tuesdays, baked bread on Wednesdays, and made a cake every Friday. Mum figured out that if we took turns we'd each bake a cake only once every three weeks. Many times we'd put a record on the victrola while we dusted the furniture and oiled the downstairs floors and then danced around as we worked, each trying to outdo the other in comic relief. Mum could be as hilarious as Dad; she often had Irene and me weak with laughter.

While Mum ran the farm, Geoff was gaining a reputation as one of the best outdoor fashion photographers in New York. He did regular work for *Vogue* and *Harper's Bazaar* magazines and got contracts for the covers and opening pages—the only ones in color—of Sears Roebuck and Montgomery Ward catalogs. From time to time, carloads of emaciated models and New York editors—called "editresses" in those days—descended on Windyridge Farm so Geoff could photograph the season's fashions against our country backgrounds. In winter Geoff and Mum left John and me and Irene on the farm while they took photography trips to Arizona. As Geoff's fame grew, he became increasingly temperamental, and jobs sometimes slipped through his fingers. At home, he was mercurial. One day you could do nothing wrong in his eyes; the next day nothing right, and you never knew why. But Geoff's problems in business weren't all his fault. As the country girded itself for war, fashion was put on a back burner.

After England and France declared war on Germany on September 3, 1939, all of us kept up on the progress of the war in Europe and argued over who'd be first to read *Life* magazine or *Reader's Digest*. In the long winter evenings during the Battle of Britain and the Blitz, we gathered around the radio, knitting balaclava helmets and scarves for Bundles for Britain. After 1941, when Congress passed the Lend-Lease

Act, America turned its attention to building jeeps, tanks, airplanes, ships, and guns and to raising food. We became part of what was called "the farm effort." Just knowing this made grading the eggs in the cool but claustrophobic egg room or picking a peck of beans in the blazing hot sun seem like important and patriotic things to do. From coast to coast, people were planting Victory Gardens. Mum said, "our whole farm is a Victory Garden."

After the Japanese bombed Pearl Harbor in December 1941 and the United States declared war, the whole country was united in a spirit of patriotism. It permeated our lives. Geoff tried to enlist in the Navy, but the recruiting officers told him he was too old. Later, after D Day, he hung a huge map on the wall and charted the movements of the Allied and Axis armies with colored pins. We never forgot we were English, but we adored our adopted country and the principles for which it stood. When we heard Kate Smith ending her Sunday-night radio shows with "Oh beautiful, for spacious skies, for amber waves of grain," we thought of our own fields of oats and wheat joined by hundreds of thousands of others from coast to coast.

The war actually helped Mum make a financial success of farming. She found out the government allowed a special tax break for family farms. To qualify you had to raise many different animals—about ten different breeds, as I recall, so one by one Mum started to accumulate them. First came the chickens, our cash crop. Next came a pedigree Guernsey calf called, symbolically, Dawn-of-a-New-Day (Dawn for short). They gave her to me, and it was my job to milk her. Unfortunately, Dawn took one look at me and decided I was not her type. She was right. I'm a sound sleeper, not readily given to leaping from a cozy bed at the crack of dawn.

When Dawn came in heat, we hauled her over to a neighbor's farm. We all sat in a row on the fence and watched while his prize young bull tried to figure out what to do about it. Eventually he caught on. In due time Dawn had her calf and thus became a cow, or "freshened" as the farmers say when a cow's milk is newly established. After that she took malicious delight in either holding back her milk or—if I'd managed to squeeze a few drops out of her—in slamming her dirty hoof into the bucket. When a farmer told us this behavior was normal for young cows, I was exonerated. We gave up on Dawn and bought a good-natured little Jersey who willingly squirted out gallons of naturally homogenized milk with a layer of thick cream that rose to the top. We had so much butter we froze some. Mum sold it to her friends when they gathered to do exercises, swap books, and have lunch.

After the cows came the sheep, so we could raise our own spring lamb. We tethered our first lamb on the lawn; as long as he lived, we didn't have to mow it. We called that first lamb George, which taught us a lesson. When a portion of his former self arrived, all crisp and juicy, on the dinner table Bill piped up with, "Is this George?" and everyone left the table in tears.

"From here on we will no longer make pets of farm animals," declared Mum. But we continued to name them. We gave our pigs the names of flowers—Pansy the fattest, Delfinium the thinnest, Sweet William, our good-natured boar, and Snap Dragon, a bad-tempered sow with menacing teeth. We didn't raise ordinary pink or white swine—not us. Ours were snooty Berkshire hogs with fancy pedigrees, round backs, fat bottoms, curly tails, and no brains. Pigs are usually intelligent, but our black beauties did everything wrong from rolling on their babies to refusing to nurse. Mum said they were her greatest challenge.

I might've gone through life thinking all pigs were stupid had not two razorback piglets escaped from a neighboring farm. One crisp fall day, John and I spotted them rooting in the middle of our corn field. The corn had already been harvested; the stubble, cut by machete, stood like rows of sharp knives. But John and I threw caution to the winds, and lit out after those piglets. They saw us coming and streaked off between the rows. John chased the big one and I went for the runt. "Tackle 'em!" he yelled as we drew close. Arms outstretched, we threw ourselves down between the rows of stubble and each caught our piglet. They squealed their heads off as we carried them by their hind feet half a mile home to the farmer who'd lost them. As a reward, the farmer gave us the runt. She grew up to be our pet pig, Flossy, trotting around the farm on our heels, sleeping in the barn, going for walks, and acting just like an extra watchdog.

Once Mum had collected the obvious animals, she branched into fowls and got a pair of everything she could think of—bantams, guinea hens, turkeys, geese, and ducks—both Pekinese and Muscovy. We also had wild pigeons in the barn, two or three dogs, two house cats, umpteen barn cats, and three bee hives. John was the beekeeper. By the time Mum had added rabbits to our Noah's Ark, I'd chopped the heads off hundreds of squawking chickens and dunked their carcasses by the feet into buckets of boiling water. I could pluck one clean in five minutes flat. You have to do things like that on a farm, but when it came to fluffy white creatures with sweet pink ears I put down my flat foot. "I'll gladly raise rabbits in cages," I said, "and feed them clover for special treats. I'll even eat them smothered in parsley sauce, but I absolutely and positively refuse to kill or skin them. John or Geoff will have to do that." It was illogical, but it passed muster; Mum and Irene felt the same way.

With all these animals wandering around and exuding the digested remains of all the corn, oats, wheat, mash, skim milk, and hay we stoked into their bellies, you can imagine how our land produced. Of course we limed our soil to keep it from becoming too acid, but the thing that made our crops and our garden grow more than any other was the chicken manure Geoff spread over all the land at least twice a year. For the most part it wasn't aged, either. When the manure spreader filled up there was usually a field that had been mowed or harvested. He'd spread it straight on and the rains washed it in. Once John had learned to run the tractor, he did most of the plowing and mowing. Geoff spread the manure and he, Baron or Buck Hovsepian, or one of our temporary hired men, did the seeding. Mum apprenticed John to a carpenter and later to a blacksmith in town. John, who was very skillful, learned how to build everything from pig styes to range houses with skids, so you could hitch them to the tractor and pull them around. Irene and I followed up with a coat of creosote.

Everything on Windyridge was neat and shipshape; all the farm structures were painted or whitewashed, often on a yearly basis. We kids did so much painting we got pretty sick of it. Mum thought she was doing John and me a favor when she put "whitewash the wall next to the cow stalls" on our TO DO lists one hot and sticky summer day. It was cool in the barn, but there were twenty cow stalls next to a concrete walk flanked by a long stone wall covered with plaster. It was a section of our barn's original foundations and supported massive beams that held up the floor of the loft. John and I knew to paint the wall's rough surface with plain water first so the whitewash would flow on quickly and smoothly, but after the first few swipes with his brush John had a brain wave.

"What do you say I throw this bucket of water at the wall?" he asked. "Then we could each take two whitewash brushes, one in each hand, and spread it around." Sounded great to me

IS ONE OF these sheep George?

and worked so well that John reached down and picked up a bucket brimming with whitewash. I gasped.

"Do you really think you should?"

"Just watch me!" he cried stepping backward several paces and taking a running start. He swung that bucket of whitewash high in the air and threw its contents toward the wall, aiming it lengthwise just below the beams at the top of the wet patch we'd already made. The white goopy stuff spread out like slow motion through the air en route to the wall, then hit it—SPLAT!—and slithered down.

"Don't just stand there grinning, dummy, CHARGE!" yelled John.

We fell on that wall with wild gusto like a couple of painters gone stark raving mad, feverishly spreading the creamy stuff around before it had time to drip down onto the floor. Of course a lot of the whitewash did hit bottom. Even more of it coated John and me. But when we'd progressed section by section down the whole wall, we threw several buckets of water on the floor and one at each other and then brushed off the floor with a broom. We finished the job in one hour instead of five and just as we were standing there admiring our work, in came Mum to see how we were doing. "My goodness, children," she exclaimed. "What a couple of speed demons you are! But it's strange that so much whitewash has ended up in the barnyard." Mum never asked how we did it; if she knew, she never let on.

Then there was school. Bill went to private school at Newtown Friends and commuted with Pearl Buck's children, who lived just over the hill to the north of us. Pearl Buck, author of *The Good Earth*, was at the height of her fame and was unfriendly. I always knew when a phone call was from Pearl Buck because you could have knocked the icicles off Mum's voice. Most people said fame had gone to her head, unlike Oscar Hammerstein, whose son Jimmy was in my class at school and who was known for his kindness. John and I went to the

Doylestown Public School that housed all grades in one nineteenth-century stone building, but after a couple of years Mum and Geoff declared John was "getting hay seed in his hair" and sent him to George School, a coeducational Quaker boarding school, for his junior and senior years.

I loved my teachers at the Doylestown school and my good friend, Virginia Lee Diver. But the best part of school was the walk back and forth to the school bus. The shortest way was through our woods, across the stream, over the hill, and through another farmer's fields. After John went to George School, I made this walk alone; prior to that we walked together. In spring it was heaven, but once in winter, after a heavy snow followed by a thaw, the stream became a raging torrent. The only way to cross it was by means of a fallen tree. It leaned at a steep angle from the edge of the pre-Revolutionary quarry that had provided the stone from which our house was built. I watched John crouch like a wild animal and climb across the fallen tree. With a whoop he leaped to safety on the other side.

"Come on!" he yelled. "It's easy." I faltered on the brink. "Hurry up!" yelled John, "or we'll be late." But this time I didn't follow.

"I can't do it, John, I'd fall in."

I turned back sadly; Mum would have to drive me to the bus. At that moment I realized I was only a tomboy, after all, not a real boy. And I was no longer an Indian. John's and my paths were beginning to diverge.

15.

The Great Organic Garden

IF OUR FARM had a crown jewel, it was the vegetable garden. We were, after all, a family of gardeners who'd become farmers, not the other way around. The vegetable garden was Geoff's special domain, and here we never questioned his judgment. Children have always known that a garden should be more than pretty; it should mean something. Geoff knew that a vegetable garden should be more than useful; it should be pretty. The place he chose was directly below the lawn, embraced by an L-shaped row of mature Winesap apple trees to the north and west. Just down the slope from the apple trees stood the old stone spring house; this he filled in, floored with concrete, and turned into a tool shed. There was a square stone-walled pond next to it fed by a spring. Geoff put me in charge of growing watercress in the pond. All I had to do was plant a handful of watercress bought at the A&P market in Doylestown and harvest it often. Geoff had planted his rows of raspberries at the top of the garden. Next to them he placed a path straight down the middle of the garden with rows branching off on both sides. He planted a bed of asparagus at the bottom of the garden and rows of marigolds, cosmos, and zinnias close to the top, so Mum would have a ready supply of cut flowers for the house.

When John and I first arrived on the farm, Geoff promised us each a little plot of our own the following year. He kept his word, but in line with his and Mum's theory of child raising, he never gave us any advice with them. The result was that though John and I spent many happy hours and days with the seed catalogs in winter drawing up plans and choosing what to plant, we chose all the wrong things. We also failed to prepare the soil adequately or water enough in dry weather. Our seeds failed to germinate or if they did, the plants straggled along, a far cry from our dreams. After one year of failure we gave up and apprenticed ourselves to Geoff. Other than his having a fit if we left a hoe out in the rain, it was a satisfactory arrangement.

Geoff had always believed in gardening the natural way, so when J. I. Rodale founded *Organic Gardening and Farming* magazine in 1942—the *Farming* has since been dropped—he became a charter subscriber. Geoff embraced Rodale's twin philosophies of organic gardening and living in harmony with nature with almost religious zeal. Geoff was given to that sort of thing. For example, when lightning cracked over the house at midnight and thunder rattled the windows and the electricity conked out, he would gather us together in the living room, and by the light of a candle, with many a dramatic flourish, read the Bible aloud. When the rain came down in sheets, he would look up toward the heavens and, in a booming voice, give thanks. It was a little embarrassing, but at least one felt that God had heard. Those were years of good rains for the most part, and our farm and garden depended on them.

Combined with our canning and the animals we raised, our vegetable garden brought Mum and Geoff's ideal of wartime self-sufficiency to fruition. In four short months of harvest, we got enough fresh produce to feed ourselves every necessary vegetable except fresh lettuce in winter. By November, our storage cellar was a sight to behold. We had three barrels of cider, a freezer full of frozen vegetables, smoked hams, bacon, and sausages hanging from the ceiling, bushels of potatoes and onions stacked in the corners, and rows of shining jars of pickles, jam, ketchup, whole tomatoes, stewed tomatoes, tomato juice, and corn covering the walls.

Mum had said that life on Windyridge Farm wouldn't be "all fun and games," but neither was it all work and slavery. We often went to the Spadeas' farm on Saturday afternoons in summer. When we did, we kids were ecstatic because we could swim in their ice-cold, spring-fed pool. We adored Jean and Jim and their three children—Sterling and Anne, who were close to our ages, and Sara the baby—and we loved the atmosphere of their farm and their happy-go-lucky lifestyle. There was also the fascinating array of guests who played bocce ball on the lawn and stayed for Jim's ratatouille and red wine at the table under the grape arbor.

William Allen White from Kansas and his vivacious wife Katherine of *Time* magazine were almost always there; they were the Spadeas' next door neighbors. A dashing war correspondent, White was a man of elegance with a twinkle in his eye, not yet sporting the monocle that so became him in his later years. The White's pretty adopted daughter Barbara, who'd lost her natural mother and father in the London Blitz and provided White with the story for his best-known book, *Journey for Margaret,* clung to the Whites in a heartrending way when she was little. She grew up to be a wonderful woman carrying on the family newspaper business. Another favorite of mine was James Michener, a gentle person, kind and quiet, often drifting away from the noisy table to sit on the porch steps alone with his thoughts, drinking in the peace and watching the twinkling fireflies.

Sometimes, on a Sunday night, I drove back to New York with the Spadeas in Jim's vintage Rolls Royce to stay for a week in their dark-brown brick house with its rickety elevator. It was two houses actually—numbers 122 and 124 East 38th Street, between Park and Lexington Avenues. It had been built by Abraham Lincoln's son, Robert Todd Lincoln, for his twin daughters. Today, it's listed among New York's historic buildings. Anne and I spent our nights sharing dreams for the future and our days haunting the art museums. At the Spadeas' Monday-night cocktail parties, I met intellectuals such as Joe Livingston, the Pulitzer Prize–winning economist, characters such as Foxy Sondheim, mother of Stephen Sondheim, and many of the best-known dress designers of that day, including the vivacious and witty Vera Maxwell, wearing black and jingling armloads of silver bracelets, and the more restrained Claire McCardell. Later, when I was in college, the much-lionized Christian Dior was there, dripping creativity from every pore. He wanted to buy one of Anne's mystical paintings—a mother with a child on her shoulder—but she said no! It was Dior who brought in the New Look that Anne and I loved—long flowing skirts with petticoats, pinched waists and wide belts that made women feel feminine again after austere wartime restrictions when designers could only use small amounts of fabric.

Every year that we lived on the farm, Dad and Margot drove all the way from California where they were living and took John and me to Pond Island for two or three blissful weeks in August. Even back on the farm, we didn't spend all our time working. One of Mum's rules was that everyone must rest and read a book after lunch for half an hour or more in hot weather. Mum also paid us for our work. I got seven dollars a week, generous for those days, and she insisted that we children get Saturday afternoons and Sunday off, not counting the small chores we all shared. Sometimes on one of my delicious afternoons off, I'd lie under the weeping willow tree on the lawn reading *Valley of Decision* or *A Tree Grows in Brooklyn*. Every time Geoff passed en route to the vegetable garden with a wheelbarrow load of manure, he gave me a dirty look.

During the years we lived at Windyridge Farm, the keenest kinds of happiness came from the simplest of pleasures. I'm not speaking of entertainment, though of course we had that in several forms—occasional movies, weekly radio shows, comic strips, magazines, and stacks of books Gran sent from England. We all had hobbies. Mum sewed; John built airplane models, carved wooden puppets, built rockets and guns that really worked. Luckily, he didn't blow himself up, but he did succeed in shooting a hole with a homemade gun through both walls of the brooder house. I painted watercolors, wrote poems and stories, and modeled things out of clay and papier-mâché. We raised tropical fish and when they died, converted our aquariums to terrariums and grew plants in our rooms. We built castles out of bales of straw and tried to build a dam across the stream. All these activities added spice to our lives, but they weren't its most magic ingredient. Life on a farm is like panning for gold in a Sierra creek. After a while you forget you're looking for treasure and shake the pan out of habit, just because you're there and it's the thing to do. It's when you're least expecting it that you just might catch a glimmer of sunshine in the pan, reach in, and pick out a real

WHEN GEOFF CULTIVATED his miles and miles of potatoes, his thoughts about weeds evidentally bordered on the savage. He was, just as Mum said in her *Vogue* article, "a born gardener." In the background, a row of beans, one of onions, and more vegetables of various kinds stretch off in the distance.

gold nugget to put in your pocket and take home. Our years at Windyridge gave me a whole bag of gold nuggets that I never could have found on the streets of a town.

There was the joy of opening one's window a crack at bedtime, seeing snowflakes falling, and waking up the next morning to find a little pile of snow on the bedroom floor and a white and silent world outdoors. When the snow melted and sleet fell and the wind howled around the house, we curled up with seed catalogs and dreamed of the gardens we were going to plant. In those days the catalogs weren't in color, but we drooled over their descriptions of vegetables and flowers just as if they were. When April came and overnight the fresh new grass in the meadow by the springhouse sprinkled itself with flowers, I was delirious with joy and one time fell on my back in the midst of them, looking up at the sky. If I had to choose the one happiest moment of my entire life, that might be it.

When at last the ground had warmed up enough, it was time to plant our Golden Bantam and Silver Queen corn. We didn't plant our sweet corn from seed. Geoff ordered the seedlings from a local nursery, and we planted them the day they arrived bareroot, bundled together, and wrapped in damp paper. Then all of us worked together making long rows of little mud puddles in the red clay soil, sticking the young corn plants into them, and muddling them up and down so there'd be no air bubbles and their roots would be coated with life-giving earth. How we babied those rows of corn, mounding the earth around the stalks, and hoeing weekly to aerate the soil and slice down weeds. And when at last the first ears of corn were ready for picking, what rejoicing there was! Geoff, at his enthusiastic best, would suggest a Saturday night barbecue out on the lawn.

"Voila! Les poulets marinés SUPERBS!" he'd chortle, throwing a row of Mum's succulent split broilers onto the grate, having first soaked them for an hour or two in red wine, oil, garlic, and herbs. "Now, gosse! Hasten down yonder path to reap the bonny CORN!" John, Bill, and I raced across the lawn and down the grassy path. The idea was to pick the corn at the last moment, peel it in haste, and throw it straight into a tub of boiling water. Mum boiled it for only three minutes; then it was done. We sat on the lawn and, along with Geoff's half-burned but yummy chicken, ate that corn in our fingers steaming hot, rolled in fresh farm butter and washed down with red wine. Geoff poured a little for "les gosse" too. Does memory fail me or was that the best corn I've ever eaten, even counting today's super-sweets?

Then, too, there was something indescribably lovely about sauntering with a basket on your arm down the path, past the drippy mulberry tree, and into the woods and struggling home with your basket overflowing with jewel-like wineberries that abounded in our woods. Or walking across the fields with Bill skipping ahead with a basket and Irene and John and Mum and me all in a row toting the longest and heaviest ladder we had and then climbing into the tall cherry tree to pick the cherries. There was only one cherry tree on our farm. Unaccountably, it grew in a hedgerow far from the house, but every year it gave us enough cherries for two of Mum's prize sour-cherry pies with all the stones left in.

One gold nugget that I picked up transcended all the others. I was alone in the woods in spring, walking aimlessly up the hill on the far side of the stream, when my eye fell on the gray bark of a common birch tree. It was just an ordinary sapling but seen against a background of freshly sprouted light-green grass, the sight was beautiful beyond belief. Just as had happened once before at Hoyle Coast when I was five or six years old, I was swept up into some inexplicable Whole, a reality beyond human reason that made everything in the world—good and bad alike—harmonious and perfect. I wanted to leap and run with joy, but as soon as I moved, the insight vanished, leaving a vivid memory that said, "That was real, not this." For a year or more when I was alone in the woods, I was filled with a combination of yearning and happiness, like being in love.

Then one day, without warning, Geoff came home from a business trip to California and said to Mum, "Sell the farm. We're moving to Hollywood."

"What!" cried Mum. "You're asking me to sell Windyridge? Just when I've built this place up and got it running so smoothly, you want me to pull up stakes! Geoff, how could you do this to me?" History was repeating itself. Once again Geoff said he was leaving, whether Mum did or not. Once again, Mum could think of no way to resist.

In June 1944, John graduated from George School. We all knew he'd soon be drafted. In August Geoff, Mum, Bill, and I bade a sad good-bye to Irene and John, who were remaining behind to close up the farm. We drove away from Windyridge forever in Geoff's brand new woody, although no one called them woodies in those days. It was a wine-colored, mahogany-panelled, oak-ribbed Oldsmobile station wagon with "hydromatic" gears.

We did not know it then, but most of our family would eventually make our homes in the West—Mum and her third husband, Bill, in San Marcos; my half-brother Bill Morris and Colleen in Oakland; John and his second (and present) wife, Dot, high on a hillside overlooking Ashland, Oregon; John's sons and grandchildren in Northern California, and Lou and our two married daughters and five grandchildren in Southern California.

Nonetheless, it was sad leaving Windyridge Farm, but there was one benefit to leaving when we did. As a family, we had accomplished this wonderful thing. Then we said good-bye at the height of the dream, before any aspect of it was tarnished. Like a young love, never consummated, Windyridge lives in my heart forever. Our farm will never change or grow old.

16.

How Geoff Made Us into Californians

WE CAME TO California for the climate—doesn't everyone? Geoff wanted to take outdoor photographs year-round. But there was another factor. Geoff got the impression he could make a fortune with a flick of his wrist. He'd bowled everyone over at a Hollywood party, and Producer David O. Selznick had promised him a flood of work. But as it turned out, life wasn't going to be quite that easy—neither in business nor in gardening. In business you had to be affable, make your deadlines, and understand Hollywood politics. In gardening you had to be unendingly faithful and understand the very climate you came here to enjoy. Soil, climate, water, plant choice, timing—you name it—they were all different from what we'd ever known before. But we didn't learn this all at once.

Once we'd left the farm and hit the Pennsylvania Turnpike, heading for California by the northern route, Geoff was ebullient, and none of us looked back. I was going to miss the country life but not the constant work. Even Mum was swept into the spirit of adventure and saved her complaints until a couple of months later, when she was forced to sell Windyridge for twenty-eight thousand dollars, too low a price, she felt, to compensate for all the improvements we'd put in. We sped westward, vying with each other to read the little rows of Burma Shave signs as Geoff's wood-paneled station wagon sped by. Despite the blazing August heat and no air conditioning in the car, America wooed us all over again, this time with her vast spaces and magestic mountains. But after seeing the Great Plains, the Rocky Mountains, and a crimson desert sunset from the foot of Castle Rock, Los Angeles with its feather-duster palm trees and threadbare lawns didn't look like much. We spent the first night in Hollywood at an old but comfortable rooming house where Geoff had stayed before. I gazed at the mangy-looking Canary Island date palm outside my window and wondered, "Why did we ever leave the farm for this?"

Just before we had left the farm, I got a letter from Dad. "Dying to see you. As soon as you get to California hop on the bus and come down to visit us. You'll love Laguna Beach. Fun bunch of kids your age." So while Mum, Geoff, and Bill house-hunted, I went to visit Dad and Maggie, as we now called her, in Laguna Beach, where they'd been living for two or three years.

Once Dad had married Maggie, in 1940, John and I never worried about him again. Maggie doted on Dad and took care of him like a mother hen. She constantly reminded him, "Now, Emma"—short for Emerson—"don't forget your glasses" or wallet or keys or whatever it was he was likely to forget. She remembered the names of their dozens of friends. She had a particular gift for handling money, so Dad let her do it. For the rest of their lives, they lived frugally but well on Dad's income and managed to travel all over the world. When they weren't traveling, Dad spent his time painting, fishing, and gardening. But in August of 1944, when I first went to visit them in Laguna, they were working in an airplane factory to help out the war effort. Maggie was saving every penny of their earnings for travel after the war.

Dad and Maggie did, however, always establish a home base. In the 1950s, they built a pleasant house in Capistrano Beach and planted a garden around it. In the sixties, they went home to England and bought a condo in Tunbridge Wells, Kent. A few years later, they moved to Malta where Dad eventually died at just under ninety years of age. Maggie sold their villa, returned to California, and bought a condo near my cousin Harriet Clay Bemus. She continued to travel until her death a few years ago, in Singapore, a city she dearly loved. But when I went to Laguna Beach to visit Dad and Maggie in August of 1944, they were still in their prime.

Geoff put me on a southbound Greyhound bus. Once it had shaken off the oil rigs nodding over the top of Signal Hill like a tribe of two-legged dinosaurs, I got a better impression of California. Funky beach towns sparkled in the sun, and rolling hills looked like giants working on their tans. Then came that first heady whiff of orange blossoms and a sea of citrus trees stretching to purple mountains in the distance. Discounting the windbreaks of glowering eucalyptus trees, it could have been a picture on an orange crate. There wasn't a speck of smog in the air and hardly a car on the road. No modern freeways or cheek-to-jowl houses that have gobbled up the California I knew then and that have changed it into something else.

Dad met me at the bus. "Marvelous to see you, love! Guess what? Just had a letter from John. Told his draft board about his model airplanes and homemade rockets and guns. Damned dangerous I used to think, but the draft board said 'In that case we won't send you to Europe as a foot soldier; we'll send you to gunnery school.'"

Good news was in keeping with the spirit of Laguna, a place that makes artists itch to grab paints and canvas and where people fill their

ABOVE When John came home on leave Dad and Maggie drove north from Laguna and we drove south and met halfway for a family picnic on a beach. Here we are from back to front and left to right: Pat, John, Dad, Mum, my friend Paula Allen, and young Bill. LEFT John with one of his anti-aircraft guns at Fort Bliss, Texas.

lives with friends and wonderful times in the sun. The first real California garden I saw was in Laguna Beach. It was love at first sight: a brick patio, a raised fish pond, a trickling fountain, a fig tree dripping with ripe fruit, a lemon tree, a red bougainvillea, a tiny lawn, all hidden away behind a brick wall like a precious pearl in an oyster. Even the wall was artistic. By omitting a brick here and there, little gaps had been left in it, so the passerby could get a glimpse of the delights within.

This is just what had happened to Dad. Down a winding path within that garden, he and Maggie had found and later rented a woodsy guest house with masses of charm and, like many houses of that era, no heat other than the fireplace. It was only a block from the beach and belonged to Mr. Gill, the local grocer. He and Mrs. Gill were away from the main house all day long, selecting fruits and vegetables for their customers and placing them fondly in brown-paper sacks. You didn't get to pick out your own apricots at Mr. Gill's open-fronted store.

A week or two later, when I returned to Los Angeles, Mum and Geoff had already bought and moved into a white Byzantine bungalow on North Crescent Heights, half a block north of Sunset Boulevard near Schwabb's Drugs. I expected Rudolph Valentino to leap from the roof onto the back of an Arabian stallion and gallop into the setting sun. But even Hollywood kitsch can have its good features—parquet floors, a walled roof for sunbathing, an interior patio, and detached maid's quarters that Mum gave to me. I filled its bare shelves with books and tacked a poster of Picasso's *Lovers* on the wall. I was happy the minute I stepped through the bedroom door, no matter what went on in the house.

Then there was the garden soil. Most soils in Southern California are poor and almost all of them are alkaline. Quite by accident, Mum and Geoff had stumbled on a place with strange-looking, loose, grayish, earth that had coarser grains than sand. Every time I walked across the bare backyard my mocassins filled up with the darn stuff. Just to look at it you wouldn't have thought it would grow a thing. Geoff and I stood side-by-side in the blazing sun and stared at it.

"Looks like a kid's sandbox with no sides," I said.

"AHA!" said Geoff crouching down and pulling up a root. "Clap your eyes on THIS, my girl! If I'm not greatly mistaken, here lie the half-rotted remains of a lowly cabBAAGE! Someone has grown veggies in this seemingly hopeless spot."

"They have indeed," said a voice from the other side of the row of eugenias that divided our yard from our neighbor's.

"Mrs. Knott!" cried Geoff jovially. "Do please step through the hedge and give us the benefit of your wise council. There's a gap over here."

Mrs. Knott popped out of the hedge like the cork from a bottle of champagne. "This ground will grow anything," she asserted, "and yes, the last owner had a vegetable garden. The soil is decomposed granite, you see. Full of minerals. In lots of places like on top of those hills it's as hard as a rock and difficult to garden in." She gestured toward the Hollywood hills; we were only a block south from one of them. It was still covered with chapparal instead of houses. "But down here,' she continued, "we're on an alluvial fan, an ancient wash from Laurel Canyon. The soil is loose and friable; it's amazing what it will grow. All you need to do is get yourself a bale or two of bean straw from one of the farmers in the San Fernando Valley. Dig the bean straw into the ground, and keep it wet. It'll rot quickly and give you all the nitrogen you need. But let me caution you—decomposed granite is like a sieve. You'll have to water constantly."

"We'll do just as you say!" cried Geoff. Water was no problem in those days; Los Angeles was awash in it—not from the skies, but out of the tap and the garden hose. "It's a damn shame we're too late to plant."

"But you still can!" laughed Mrs. Knott. "Early September is the perfect time to put in vegetables here. The whole trick is knowing what to plant when. You see, in Southern California we grow vegetables year-round, but we grow the cool-season crops in winter and the warm-season ones in summer. You've got to wait until spring to plant the things that love hot weather like tomatoes, green beans, corn, eggplants, squash, cucumbers, and melons. But you can put in all cabbage crops now and other things that like cool weather, like lettuce, peas, celery, and parsley. You can also plant carrots, radishes, beets, chard, or turnips any time all year and a few things like potatoes either in spring or fall."

"Wondrous news, my dear Mrs. Knott! Lucky WE, to have settled next to such a helpful soul as THOU!" Geoff breathed down her neck and laid on charm with a trowel. Half-amused, she took a step back and smoothed out her apron.

"Another thing I recommend is that you put in a row of stock for Mrs. Morris," she said primly. "They're so fragrant, and they grow extremely well here if you plant them now," Then she popped back through the hedge as quickly as she'd appeared. Mrs. Knott's garden was a mixed jungle containing all the usual Hollywood plants of that era—pittosporum, bird-of-paradise, oleander, hibiscus, jasmine, a few roses, an orange tree, a lemon tree, a loquat, a Washingtonia fan palm, a smattering of cacti and succulents, and a gawky row of poinsettias next to the garage. Her husband spent his weekends chopping things back.

Strange as some of Mrs. Knott's instructions sounded, we followed them to the letter. We dug in the bean straw, and planted beets, broccoli, carrots, cauliflower, celery, lettuce, onions, parsley, peas, radishes, Swiss chard, spinach, a few potatoes, and a row of stock. We watered often, and everything grew like mad. Geoff and I congratulated each other on our success and were ready to try something else.

"If we want to be real Californians," he announced one day, "we should plant a eucalyptus tree." All four of us—Geoff, Mum, Bill, and

I were lying on our backs on an old plaid blanket in the shade of a giant eucalyptus, having just finished one of Geoff's famous French picnics. It was "Bloody MAAHVELOUS," as he himself had declared.

Geoff's picnic method was simple. First, he spread out the old plaid blanket and then on top of it he tossed a loaf of French bread, a bread knife, a bottle of red wine, a Coke for Bill, a whole smoked German sausage, a quarter pound of butter, half a dozen whole tomatoes, a few hard-boiled eggs, a hunk of Vermont extra-sharp white cheddar—during the war you couldn't get Brie—some apples, and a slab of chocolate. By the time we'd finished the first course and were polishing off the chocolate on top of slices of buttered French bread—Geoff always claimed this was better than cake—and swilling it down with the last of the wine, Mum and I were in the mood for agreeing with anything, even to drippy eucalyptus trees. So the minute we'd dropped off Mum and Bill at home, Geoff and I took off in the car again, this time to the local nursery.

Neither he nor I knew that there were more than five hundred species of eucalyptus growing wild in Australia or that approximately a hundred, including hybrids, were cultivated in California and that each of these had widely differing characteristics. But when we asked for a eucalyptus, the nurseryman swept all that aside. "This is what you want then," he said and showed us a row of skinny blue gums, the kind I'd seen as windbreaks in Orange County. They were growing in gallon cans and already three feet tall. "Great!" said Geoff. "We'll take two."

That very day we planted those trees, one on each side of the fish pond flanking the front window. The minute we stuck them in the ground, they began shooting to the sky. When John arrived by bus from Pennsylvania en route to basic training at the anti-aircraft school in Fort Bliss, Texas, he couldn't believe they'd already doubled in size. But they had—or close to it. None of us had ever seen anything grow so fast.

"It's miraculous!" exclaimed Geoff. "Amazing!" agreed Mum. Mrs. Knott kept her mouth shut, and by spring we understood why. Our two eucalyptus trees had reached the roof, killed the lawn, and sprinkled its remains with dead leaves, buttons, and twigs. Next, they pushed up the flagstones in the entrance way, stopped up our sewer pipes, sneaked up the drainage holes of all our flower pots, and strangled our geraniums. Thus we learned our first three rules of California gardening—don't plant something just because it grows fast because the fastest-growing plant is seldom the best; do look things up before you choose them; and never plant an invasive eucalyptus tree near your house or where you want to grow anything else.

John had been given ten days to proceed to base, time enough to help Geoff make the garage into a darkroom and chase round to drugstores for Mum because there was a shortage of cigarettes. On the weekend we drove south toward Laguna Beach and met Dad and Maggie half way for a family picnic. There we were, all together on a rocky beach—Dad, Maggie, Geoff, Mum, John, Bill, me, and the daughter of an English vaudevillian called Paula Allen, a friend I'd met at Hollywood High.

Driving west to California I'd had plenty of time to imagine what Hollywood High was going be like, but the real thing was better. Great teachers, lovely buildings, indoor swimming pool, huge auditorium, playing fields, lawns, ubiquitous palms, flower beds, and a student body of friendly, talented kids. I'd also made up my mind that when I went to Hollywood High I was going to come out of my shell, smile at everyone, make lots of friends, and stop scowling—a habit I'd gotten into during the years I was outwardly a small girl but inwardly an Indian brave. "You grew up overnight," said Mum. "I've never seen anything like it. One day you were a child, and the next day you were a woman to be reckoned with. We were all so surprised." On the farm I never knew what was going on. When we reached Hollywood I woke up and realized that our family was far from idyllic. Geoff got drunk and angry almost every evening, and Mum, whom I'd always thought of as a paragon, was more like a Greek goddess with very human faults to balance all her virtues. In my teenage opinion these two talented, charismatic people hadn't the vaguest idea of how to get along with each other, let alone bring up Bill. "I have a suggestion," I told them when they asked me to mediate their frequent fights, "Why don't you take turns giving in?" I also woke up to the fact that, despite Bill's expensive private schooling, no one ever taught him how to read, so I taught him.

Then came the rains. The skies opened, the waters fell, the streets flooded, the traffic snarled; you'd think it had never rained before. Our vegetables loved it. We were soon picking enormous heads of broccoli and romaine. The stock spread out sideways and became sturdy giants before they'd even begun to bloom. But people got soaked to the skin. It was evidentally un-Californian to own a raincoat or carry an umbrella. At school the kids threw jackets and notebooks over their heads and dashed across the flooded quad. Rain or no rain, Hollywood High of that era was a kind of heaven for me, but at home all hell broke loose.

First, the walled sun roof filled up like a swimming pool, gave way in the middle of the night, and collapsed on the foot of Mum and Geoff's bed. Mum had an instant nervous breakdown—you couldn't blame her—she went to bed in another room, and wasn't talking. When I came in from my snug castle, having slept soundly through the crisis, the doctor had just left. Mrs. Knott was in the hall. She said, "You run the house, Pat, and cook for Geoff and Bill. I'll take care of your mother and bring her all her meals." Mum stayed in bed for a month and never spoke. Then one afternoon she got up. When I came home from school she was cooking dinner as if nothing had ever happened.

According to Mum's penciled notes, which I have recently found, it took her a while longer to recover completely. The rains stopped, the sun came out. I continued to run the house, and Mum spent a month or two reading and sunbathing on the newly repaired roof. Then one day she suddenly felt better. "I've decided to open an antique shop in the two front rooms of Geoff's studio on the Sunset Strip," she told me. Geoff's business was going from bad to worse. Once again—just as she had done when she bought the farm—Mum had conceived of a way to keep the family afloat. In a week or two she and Geoff were warring again like Hera and Zeus, but Mum had her store.

One day Mrs. Knott called me into her kitchen and said, "They're all crazy in that house, Pat, and if you don't escape you'll go crazy, too. Here's the phone number of the Girl Scout headquarters. Go on down there and apply for a summer job as a counselor at Camp Osito in the San Bernardino mountains. Tell them you can do anything, that you learned how on the farm." I was going to be sixteen in May, too young to be a counselor, but Leo, the camp director, found a way to hire me. She made me assistant to the arts and crafts counselor. In June I packed up and left.

The arts and crafts counselor was Charlene Lamb, Ching for short. After a short conversation, we began to laugh. Neither one of us had ever done any of the crafts we were going to teach, but both of us thought there was nothing we couldn't do. We figured things out at night, and the next day taught the kids. Gales of laughter erupted from the craft hut all summer long. It was the beginning of a lifelong friendship with Ching and her husband Jim, who at that time was in the Navy serving in the Pacific. By mid-summer the war had ended. Dad and Maggie left and went back to England for a visit. On the way home, they stopped in Bermuda and stayed for two years.

As if enough hadn't happened already, one month after Ching and I arrived at Camp Osito, a forest fire broke out. Whipped by Santa Ana winds, it headed straight for the camp. I was detailed to ride one of the horses down the hill. As I raced toward the stables, I saw a whole tree explode in flames. Fortunately, the wind changed, and the camp was saved. Everyone was evacuated and told to return in a week. I arrived home in Hollywood by public bus late Saturday afternoon, alone, with little money in my pockets, covered with dirt and smoke, and dog-tired. I hadn't slept in thirty-six hours. When I looked through the front window of our house, I received the shock of my life. The house was empty. Not a stick of furniture, no packing boxes, nothing.

Thoroughly shaken, I sat down on the doorstep to think. Mrs. Knott was away and so was my civics teacher, Mrs. Halliday, who lived in the next block. All my closest friends were on vacation. Luckily I remembered a schoolmate of Bill's who lived only a few blocks away. With the help of his family and telephone information, I found Mum and Geoff in Inglewood, ten miles south of Hollywood. They'd run out of money, sold our house, and rented a tract house. I took the bus to Inglewood, and Geoff picked me up at the bus stop. Mum met me at the door and said, "I sent you a postcard saying we'd moved." I felt she and Geoff had no concept of what I'd been through, but maybe I was wrong. Years later, Mum told me she had never believed in apologizing to her children. "It would give them the upper hand," she said. She'd fixed a wonderful dinner, but before she could put my plate in front of me I was sound asleep.

Tract houses in those days were not what they are today. They formed row after row of identical little stuccoed boxes, each with a garage glued on one side and an asbestos-tile roof plunked on top. They had been thrown up in great haste to solve the housing problem. Ours was across from a bean field, near the Los Angeles airport. We lived there for two years. "Our low ebb" Mum called it. Meanwhile, Bill was a boarder at Chadwick School in Rolling Hills; John was a technical sergeant in the

TOP My senior picture.
ABOVE The south lawn of Hollywood High, where I often had lunch, flanked Sunset Boulevard.

army of occupation in Japan; and I still went to Hollywood High, commuting back and forth with Geoff. My room looked out on a backyard surrounded by a brown fence, just short enough to allow ourselves and our neighbors, none of whom we knew, to see each other's heads bobbing up and down when we mowed our lawns. You couldn't even sit in the shade of the pathetic cluster of castor bean plants that leaned over the cracked cement patio without feeling a stranger's eyes staring at you. My room at the back of the house had been my only sanctuary, except when Mum had gone back to England to visit Gran and Grandad and buy antiques. For those blissful six months, at the end of my senior year in high school, I'd stayed in Nichols Canyon in Hollywood with Mr. and Mrs. Russell Hicks. Mrs. Hicks was a retired actress. Russell was a movie actor who'd taken the parts of generals, politicians, and businessmen in dozens of films. Currently, he was "between pictures." They had four daughters and said one more wouldn't hurt.

In June 1947 I graduated from Hollywood High and spent the summer finishing antiques for Mum's antique store. In September, filled with happy enthusiasm and eagerness for the future I started to pack the old trunk that had carried my things between Yorkshire and Rickmansworth and later to America. With the help of a scholarship, a job as a dining-room waitress, some money from Dad's estate, and Mum's strong backing against Geoff's opposition, I was going to Scripps College. It wasn't the first time I'd flown the nest, but I knew that this time Mum hated to see me go; maybe she was even a little jealous. Ever since we'd left the farm, she'd counted on me to help her just like Irene had once done. Many years later, just before her ninetieth birthday after which she suddenly died, Mum told me how much my help had meant to her. In the old days, she never would have admitted it—she was far too proud for that.

I opened the creaking lid of my trunk and lined the bottom of it with a few of my favorite books—Wordsworth, Robert Frost, and *1066 and All That*—when Mum came to the door of my room. She handed me a black and white antique jug. "Here," she said. "You'll need something to put flowers in, so take this." Mum knew there was a cutting garden for the students at Scripps so we could pick flowers for our rooms. "Pack it in the middle with your sweaters," she added, "so it won't break. The base of the handle is cracked right through. Otherwise we wouldn't have it any more, would we?" And we both laughed, because the little jug would have been sold by now, like everything else in her antique shop.

The shop, called Morris of London, was right across from La Rue's restaurant and next to Allen Adler, the silversmith, a prime location. Mum had started by selling all the lovely antiques we'd brought from England, from the Cromwellian sideboard to our best Queen Anne teapot. It was difficult at first to part with our treasured possessions, but after a while we got into the spirit of it. As Mum pointed out, we had to eat. We were excited when Jennifer Jones bought several things and said she'd tell her friends. Geoff had taken publicity photos of her for *Duel in the Sun.* (His photos were a hit; it was just his luck the movie wasn't.) We were proud when Lauren Bacall and Humphrey Bogart—Bogie and Baby they called each other—were among our best customers. Mum and I took heart and began spending some of the money to buy new things. Despite gas rationing, we traveled as far as San Diego on buying trips. I thought some of the things she bought were junk. "Never mind," she said. "We'll fix them up." We became expert refinishers, washing the old finishes off with lye and hot water, rinsing and drying and sanding and then applying coat after coat of the finest varnish and rubbing down each thin dry layer with fine sandpaper or steel wool.

I still have the little soft-paste antique jug that Mum gave to me that day when I was packing for college. On the bottom it says "Farmers Arms" and under that "B and L." The crack in the handle is clearly visible. On

ABOVE Part of Mum's display at the Los Angeles Antique Show. It was a little sad to see our Cromwellian sideboard (left rear), Mum's desk that she used at the farm (center), and our Georgian silver tea pot (middle shelf, just right of center) up for sale.
RIGHT Front view of the antique jug Mum gave me the day I packed for college.

PHOTO BY MELINDA HOLDEN

one side, a banner intones "GOD SPEED THE PLOUGH." Above that are the farmer's wife and her butter churn across from the farmer, who is lifting a glass of ale to toast his animals—pigs, chickens, ducks, cows, geese, horses—and all manner of farm impliments—sickles, scythes, rakes, clippers, spades, and a plow in the center. On the reverse side there's a banner proclaiming "INDUSTRY PRODUCETH WEALTH." Above it is this poem:

> Let the wealthy and great
> Roll in splendour and state
> I envy them not, I declare it
> I eat my own Lamb
> My own Chickens and Ham
> I shear my own fleece and I wear it.
> I have Lawns, I have Bowers
> I have Fruits, I have Flowers
> The Lark is my morning Alarmer
> So Jolly Boys now
> Here's God Speed the Plough
> Long Life and Success to the Farmer

Here was the whole essence of Windyridge Farm. A grain of it is with me still. No, I don't keep farm animals or churn butter anymore. Lou and I are far from self-sufficient, but I still like to walk outside my front door, wander down the path, and come back with an armload of vegetables for our supper. There's a certain joy in it, a peaceful rhythm of keeping in touch with Mother Earth and in tune the seasons. And although I no longer feel the ecstatic exhilaration that I was so lucky to feel when I was a child and alone in nature, I can still catch a glimpse of it in my garden.

Mum said this jug wasn't valuable. I can understand why for her that was true. But I treasure it, crack and all. When Mum gave it to me she handed me a legacy, and in my way I carry it on.

DEALING WITH DROUGHT

17.

A Dry Garden and a Blind Date

W HEN I FIRST came to West Los Angeles, I was struck by its artificiality. Beverly Hills and Bel Air seemed like a massive stage set, gardens and all. Hollywood was more real but had lived so hard and fast that it grew old before its time. You passed a wrought-iron gate and would catch a glimpse of Mediterranean magnificence—a semi-decayed landscape with formal box hedges and a marble nymph pouring water into a tile fountain—and wonder if you'd bumbled through a time warp and stepped into imperial Pompeii. But many of the newer gardens were recreations of places with plentiful rainfall such as Hawaii or England. Something was out of kilter. An abundance of imported water had created an all-green scene that fought with what California really was—a very dry place.

Sometimes I felt like a lost soul. Mother Nature had disappeared, and I was an orphan. Only when I walked away from our home on North Crescent Heights and climbed up the firebreak that creased the ridge of the Hollywood Hills far above the city did I have an inkling that nature was still around. If I just looked hard enough I might find her again—probably in the desert. I was used to the streams and forests of the East Coast and the moist climate of England. Here was the paradox. Everything in me loved the plants that needed regular irrigation in order to grow. Everything in me wanted to be surrounded by a verdant landscape—lawns, bowers, fruits, flowers—but instinct told me another approach would fit this place better.

In Southern California of the 1940s there were no restraints, no real guidelines to taste in gardening or anything else. Mme. Gana Walska's Lotusland in Santa Barbara, an inspired phantasmagoria of weird plants and theatrical displays that she began in 1941, is a perfect example of the spirit of the age. People could do anything they wanted, and no one raised an eyebrow. There were streets in West Los Angeles where every imaginable garden style from every country of the world rubbed elbows with every other. Good or bad, there was something innately attractive about all this youthful exuberance, but it was also confusing. It took me several years to sort through my conflicting thoughts and feelings and begin to develop an enduring love for Southern California. Driving across the continent, not once, not twice, but a total of seven times made me see the place with new eyes.

I was a freshman at Scripps when Mum and Geoff finally got fed up with Hollywood. They suddenly pulled up stakes, moved back to Pennsylvania and sank their last remaining bit of capital into Woodhill, the house they owned during my college years. They left Hollywood because Geoff's movie-oriented photography business had completely dried up, and Mum's antique shop didn't make enough money to take its place. Fortunately, Geoff's old contacts in the New York fashion industry were glad to have him back. But by leaving, Mum and Geoff upset the applecart of my college financing. Mum and I had figured everything out to the penny. There wasn't anything extra for traveling back and forth by plane or train across the country. I couldn't spend my vacations with Dad and Maggie because they were still living in Bermuda, and Mum and Geoff believed in the Spartan ideal. Children weren't supposed to ask for more money or even advice; when problems came along and situations changed, they were supposed to work things out for themselves.

It turned out to be easier than I thought. Every summer, except one time when I took a Greyhound bus across the country, I discovered someone with a car who wanted to drive home to the East Coast, sharing expenses and the wheel with three other students. We often camped out en route and sometimes zigzagged across the country to stop at national parks or stay with friends and relatives. In an era of cheap gas, twenty-five cent hamburgers, and three-dollar-a-night motels, the entire journey cost less than thirty dollars apiece and took eight to ten days. These six adventuresome cross-country trips provide a sort of framework for my memories of four intensely happy college years.

In June of 1948, after my freshman year in college, four of us headed east in a black, air-conditioned Cadillac on Route 66. Except when I was driving, I sat in the back, gazing out the window as usual. It wasn't like freeway travel. You could reach out, touch the land, and feel America's pulse. As you drove by on the narrow two-lane road, bare deserts sang their stories to you and so did wooded mountains, endless plains, muddy rivers, dirty cities, and small towns that time had passed by. The very hugeness of the country was enthralling. The sheer monotony of the plains bound you in sympathy to the pioneers.

At last came western Pennsylvania. We topped a hill and as our car wound down the other side it was as if we'd entered the tropics. Green vines and trees dripping over the rocky escarpment on both sides caused a whooshing sound as we drove through the deep-cut road. I rolled down the window to hear the sound better and drink in the silky air, fragrant with wet foliage from a recent shower. Here was the exuberance I adored; nature untamed, proud, luxuriant, overwhelming the works of man with so much growth no highway maintenance crew could keep up with it. The rains fell and the green growth grew. This is what I must have, I thought. This is me. But I was in for a surprise.

I went alone into the woods that summer, up onto Jericho Mountain. What great names there were near Woodhill—Jericho Mountain, Eagle Road, Egypt Farm, Snake Lane. I walked up Eagle Road like a girl going back to an old flame, expecting to be swept up into his arms, but to my dismay the magic was no longer there. We'd grown apart. The woods, pantheism, Wordsworth's *Tintern Abbey*, mystical nature—where had they all flown? Somewhere out in Hollywood I'd lost all that. But when fall came and my three traveling companions and I drove west again in the same old black Cadillac, I began to discover it wasn't lost, only misplaced. We shook off the old, green, established places. We made our way once more in the tracks of the pioneers across the plains. And then came the dry west. The vast, free, magnificent spaces. What a revelation! This is where I belonged after all.

The first California garden I'd seen, the one surrounding Mr. Gill's guest house in Laguna Beach, had felt real. It was never watered more than once a week, if that. Gradually I began to realize that there were other gardens that felt real to me too, and they were the drier gardens created by people who set limits upon themselves and grew plants in tune with lower water use. It wasn't necessary for these gardens be filled with native plants, although great California natives like ceonothus and Matilija poppy could often be found there. These gardens didn't even look dry; they were often highly colorful and lush in appearance. The quality that set them apart was the choice of plants that grew in them—bougainvillea, lantana, aloes, tea trees, pride of Madiera, cup-of-gold, and dozens of other plants that hailed from places in the world with climates similar to our own. Once well-established, they didn't need their roots soaked with water to live. Your main task was to tide them over between the rains.

My husband Louis was living in just such a natural California garden when I first met him. I'd always taken it for granted that I would someday marry a fellow gardener. It didn't surprise me at all that my future husband was living in a gardener's cottage located in a wild and enchanting garden. It seemed totally fitting.

Lou's cottage was hidden along with three others in a canyon behind a house on Kearsarge Street in Brentwood. The house belonged to a Mrs. Fargo who rented the cottages. The former owner had planted a forest of eucalyptus trees in the canyon behind the main house. When Mrs. Fargo and her late husband had bought the place, they envisioned it as an excellent spot for creating a little extra income. The Fargos hired laborers to dig wide terraces on the sides of the canyon and a steep trail connecting them and winding down to the bottom. They surfaced the trail with bucketfuls of rough concrete poured on the ground and flattened slightly with a hoe. On the terraces they built four cottages of pine clapboards with open beams and shingle roofs. They painted the cottages flat white indoors and out. Each cottage had a foundation and fireplace of red brick and each one was completely hidden from all the others by vines, trees, and shrubs. Lou's place had a bathroom, a tiny kitchen, a back porch, and one main room with a double bed that folded down from the wall. It exuded charm, and Lou always said I married him in order to live there.

After the cottages were finished, Mrs. Fargo, an avid gardener, planted a wild landscape concentrating on plants that would survive with little care. In the early years, she watered and tended her canyon. As she grew old, she rarely went down there, and the place became a jungle existing mainly on winter rains and its own refuse. The eucalyptus trees had gone deep into the ground to find water. Thus satisfied, they never made a mat of surface roots. The canyon had never been scraped off or gouged out by a bulldozer, so the soil was deep and loamy, full of organics and covered with a thick layer of rotting leaves. Two of the cottages had shaggy bermuda lawns dependent on the good graces of renters to squirt some water at them occasionally and attack them with a rickety mower. Then there were masses of geraniums, great drifts of naked ladies, giant agaves, and cascades of blue plumbago weaving through yellow broom.

Among all these drought-resistant plants, an incongruous shrubbery of pink hydrangeas existed on runoff from Mrs. Fargo's flower beds and vegetable garden. Some slopes were covered with purple bougainvillea and others by ivy. The flat brick walk to Lou's front door was secluded behind a row of sapote trees—another incongruous touch—completely overgrown with the invasive but breathtaking perennial morning glory, known as Blue Dawn Flower. At the far end, beneath a large window and surrounded on three sides by a vine-covered picket fence, was Lou's tiny lawn, just the spot for sitting in the sun to read a book or listen to the birds. Nature had moved into this garden, settled down, and set up housekeeping. Way down in the bottom of the canyon there was even a compost heap.

Mrs. Fargo also rented garage space for three cars. When Lou arrived, there was no room in the garage for his new black Chevy convertible. That's how we met. Lou had knocked on neighbors' doors until he found a garage he could rent from a young couple half a block further up the street. That couple happened to be my old friends Ching and Jim Lamb. His renting a garage from the Lambs soon led to friendship. The three of them became involved in politics, reading books together, getting together for dinner, and staying up late laughing, talking, and discussing. Like most couples who have a close friend who is a bachelor, Ching and Jim eventually became matchmakers. Lou resisted with all his might. He'd lost more good friends this way than he could count. Every married couple he knew wanted to marry him off. When he didn't follow through after the first date and ask the girl out again, his friends would get mad at him. The last person a thirty-year-old man could imagine falling for was a college girl.

Eventually, however, fate took a hand. Gert and Henry Bristol came to Los Angeles on business, phoned me on a Saturday and invited me to come into town on Sunday to have lunch with them at the Ambassador Hotel. When lunch was over, I wasn't in the mood for going back to studying so I dropped by to visit Ching and Jim.

"What a coincidence," said Ching. "We were just talking about you! We've been wanting to have you over. How about next weekend? We have a group of married couples we get together with once a month. Saturday there's a dance. Jim and I can fix up a blind date with you and a young lawyer we know—a bachelor. Nothing romantic, of course. Just a lark, but this guy has a great sense of humor."

So the following Saturday night, I was sitting in the back of Ching's and Jim's station wagon next to Lou, whom I'd just met, and breathing in the heavy scent of gardenias. Lou had given me three of them in a corsage, and Ching had pinned it to the silk dress I'd worn to so many parties in Yorkshire and France two summers earlier when my brother John and I had returned to Hoyle Court. Until now I'd thought the scent of gardenias was cloying, but I must have been mistaken. Yes, the scent was strong, even sensual, but so much the better. All of a sudden I couldn't get enough of it.

Lou took my hand—I felt a jolt of electricity—and he continued to hold it in his warm one while talking to Ching and Jim. When we got to our destination, I joined all the wives in a tour of the house, but Lou followed me with an hors d'oeuvre. We sat on a flowered couch and told each other our life stories. We talked about books, art, Plato, our philosophies of life, our families; we even touched on food and cooking, but strangely enough, we never discussed gardening. We had so much in common Lou said with a laugh, "Shall I propose now or wait?"

"Now's fine," I answered, but to me it was no laughing matter. I meant it.

For the next week, I was wide awake at five every morning, filled with a strange excitement. I floated on air all day. I was head-over-heels in love. Before it happened, I used to wonder if falling in love was just a romantic myth and might never happen to me. Now I knew it was real.

The dance that Ching and Jim took us to that evening was at the Del Mar Club on the oceanfront in Santa Monica. Everyone signed the guest book—Mr. and Mrs. This and Mr. and Mrs. That—so Lou said, "Ha, ha! I might as well do the same!" He signed it "Mr. and Mrs. Louis M. Welsh."

Next they gave all the ladies raffle tickets so they could raffle off a bottle of champagne, and Lou said, "Well, Pat, if you win the champagne it will be the first bottle at our wedding." I won the champagne. Lou went up to claim the bottle, and when he brought it back to our table everyone cried "Open it up!" One of the men reached out to grab it. "Oh no you don't!" said Lou, snatching it away from him. "That's going to be the first bottle at our wedding!" And so it was.

We were married six weeks later on the day I graduated from Scripps. I graduated in one garden, and we were married in another. The gardeners had grown tubs of yellow marguerites for the graduation, and they simply moved them into the Memorial Garden for our small family wedding. Dr. Blaisdell, President Emeritus of Pomona College, performed the ceremony. Ching was Matron of Honor, and Jim was Best Man. Mum flew out from Pennsylvania, and John came down

LOUIS AND I
on our wedding day,
June 8, 1951, in the
Margaret Fowler
Memorial Garden at
Scripps College with
Dr. Arnold Blaisdell,
President Emeritus
of Pomona College
and Founder of the
Claremont Colleges,
who performed the
ceremony.

from Berkeley. Afterward we had dinner at a local restaurant. My cousin Harriet who was living with Dad and Maggie in the house they'd built in Capistrano Beach had made us a magnificent English wedding cake—three layers of solid fruit cake covered with marzipan and elegantly decorated with white boiled icing. She'd topped it with a circle of gardenias.

A strange thing happened at our wedding. When Dad took hold of that first bottle of champagne—the one I'd won the night Lou and I met—the bottle exploded, and the top of it broke off in Dad's hand. "Well, I never!" he exclaimed. "Someone in the kitchen must have left this bottle standing on a hot stove." It was a clean break; there was not a single splinter, so Dad poured the champagne straight out of the broken bottle. People said it was good luck, but Lou and I said it was like the glass that the groom breaks under his shoe at a Jewish wedding. In the greater scheme of things, we thought, we were meant to stay together through thick and thin.

We honeymooned for two or three days at the Hotel Bel-Air. Lou, a trial lawyer for the Santa Fe Railroad, had a case beginning Monday morning. Then we went home to our gardener's cottage hidden in the canyon behind Mrs. Fargo's house on Kearsarge Street. We'd decided to live in that cottage the day after we met. Ching had invited Lou over for breakfast, and after that he took all of us to see a Frank Lloyd Wright house he was thinking of buying. It was perfect spot for a bachelor—small, flamboyant, romantic, cantilevered at a dramatic angle high above a steep slope just off Tigertail in Brentwood.

"This place would never do for us," I said. "The babies would fall off the balcony. Anyway there's no space for a garden!"

"Okay," said Lou, and he took me to see his little house in the woods. "I suppose if I marry you I'll have to find another place for us to live."

"Why?" I asked. "I have very few possessions, and there's plenty of room for two. I can't imagine a more perfect spot."

That was that, but there's still more to the story. About a week before our wedding, I exclaimed to Lou, "Won't it be fun when we garden together on weekends!" You'd think I'd dropped a ton of bricks. "Hey wait a minute!" said Lou. "I hate gardening! I always have, and I always will."

"But you live in a gardener's cottage, so I thought . . ."

"That I was a gardener. Well, I'm a garden lover, you see, not a gardener. There's a difference. I love the results, but I don't like doing the work. You can hire a professional gardener if you want. As for me, I'd rather live in an apartment than have to do the work myself. And while we're having this discussion I'd better tell you the same goes for plumbing, electricity, carpentry, and masonry. Hire whatever help you need, but I'm all thumbs with hammers and saws. I'm just not a handyman around the house."

"Suits me fine," I said. "I learned to do all that stuff on the farm. In fact I like fixing things better than housework, but I hate sewing. I get all tangled up and frustrated, so don't expect me to do a lot of mending or darning. I'm an outdoorsy person who can't stand being cooped up in a house."

Previously, I'd visualized a marriage in which I and my mate would garden together in domestic bliss like Adam and Eve—wearing more than fig leaves of course. Now that life had turned out differently, I discovered I liked it even better. On weekends Lou and I went for walks together, read books aloud, or went to the beach and bodysurfed on the waves. And during the week I gardened in my own way. I could plant things where and when I wanted, design the garden in whatever style I wished, try out new techniques and succeed or fail without fear of criticism. Failure, after all, is often a better way to learn than success.

Whatever I decided to do with the garden was fine with Lou. I loved the work—to me it was a creative task—and Lou always admired the final results. Thus our garden became a special place we both enjoyed each in our own way.

As the years went by, my garden gave me more than pleasure. Eventually, it gave me a way to help others find pleasure in theirs. This is not to imply that I have or ever have had a perfect garden where everything looks good all the time and everything works. Far from it, for a garden is like life itself—not all easy, often a struggle, but nonetheless offering moments of contentment, triumph, or exhilaration. For those who have a garden, it's one way to be attentive to the Earth and take part in the dance of life.

Born into a family of garden lovers in Yorkshire,
England, Pat Welsh spent her teen years on a Pennsylvania
farm until her family moved west in 1945. Pat's love of
gardening eventually led to a career as a garden lecturer,
writer, and television communicator.
She lectured at garden clubs and the UCSD Extension,
and when *San Diego Home/Garden* was founded in 1979,
she became its first Garden Editor. She later spent five
years as the Emmy award-winning "Resident Gardener"
on the San Diego NBC station. The author of the
acclaimed *Pat Welsh's Southern California Gardening*,
Pat has written dozens of magazine articles and columns on
local gardening. She is the host of how-to
videotapes for *Better Homes & Gardens*. Her work has won
several gardening awards, including four
Quill and Trowel Awards from the Garden Writers of
America. Above all, she is a Southern California gardener
with her hands in the soil.